The Wondering Life

By

Colleen Cherwinski

This book is a work of non-fiction. Names and places have been changed to protect the privacy of all individuals. The events and situations are true.

ISBN: 1-4140-2570-X (e-book)
ISBN: 1-4140-2569-6 (Paperback)

Library of Congress Control Number: 2003098515

This book is printed on acid free paper.

Printed in the United States of America
Bloomington, IN

1stBooks - rev. 02/13/04

To the pain,

And the way things used to be...

If you could drift as a feather around this world,

And you could choose just one simple life to follow,

Would it be mine?

One day I woke to find that I was dying. It was not the type of dying that means I would not exist physically, but instead, inside I was dying. The inner core of me was rotting and I was slowly fading into the environment around me. On that same day, I woke to find that I had lost control of my life. I fell into darkness as I tried to pinpoint the exact moment I lost feeling of life in my body. So I began to write and when I began to write my life started. For the first time I looked my life square in the face and examined the contents underneath.

This is it.

This is the part I haven't revealed.

This is my hiding place.

These are the tears I have shed.

All the moments when I broke down and fell.

The part you missed so casually.

The constellations of my soul.

These are my dreams.

These are the things I never said.

All my fake smiles.

All my empty moments.

Every happy time.

This is my joy and my relief.

This is the fear and dread.

These are the years I have lived.

This is the truth about my life.

This is when I just come out and say it.

Do you know how I feel?

This is a road that I must walk alone,

And I am scared.

Have you ever woke up in a morning,

To find you have been living a lie?

This is my morning.

I am ashamed of myself,

Because I am exposing myself for the first time.

I think about my friends and family.

I don't want to hurt them.

But I will not hide anymore.

I will not be a coward.

But this hurts,

Because this is the first time I have ever cared about anything,

And I have waited so long.

I'm sorry for everything.

I'm sorry I waited this long to tell you the truth.

I have no faith, no courage, no love, no hope, no enthusiasm.

I am not dead,

But I am not alive.

I am the air and the sky.

I am the fog and the gleam of sliver when it rains.

Is it possible to be nothing at all?

I am in something, something bigger than I. It seems I am in a state of mind of which I cannot even begin to describe. I am losing self and hope all together. I took a walk in the early morning hours and sat in my driveway. I cried to the gentle wind that surrounded me because I believe I am hopeless.

I asked the sky why I was unable to smile the way I used to.

I asked God why I was even here at all.

I knew that no one would tell me.

I knew this was something I had to do alone.

There is a journey before me that I know I must walk. No, I'm not sure what is at the end but I know it is time I began. I need to do this because I need to live. I need to do this because I need to know who I am. These are the rights of every human in this world.

And so I begin.

Sometimes I remember my voice. Bright and clear, like it's never has been for such a long time. It used to be so loud. It said what it meant.

But it has been so long since I have heard my voice.

Silent was I for so long.

How long will I have to wait to be understood and loved if I'm silent?

I want to speak. I want to scream and cry and tell you why I am feeling the way I am today.

Just once could I say what I truly mean?

Silence is always around. I want to break it down around me. I want my voice to echo off every ear.

Just once.

Excuse me?

I think I have got something to say.

Ordinary people walk around this world,

Completely unnoticed,

Completely unappreciated.

They work Monday through Sunday and get paid minimum wage.

They buy their clothes on the sale racks.

They buy their groceries with coupons.

They budget their money, but every week they look to see no more money left in their pockets. They can't afford to have the things they truly want. They watch the television and go to the cheap Sunday movie at the theater. Sometimes when I go shopping I go into the really expensive stores just so I can look at the clothes I can never have.

Maybe that's the American dream,

Buying it all and having it all.

I realize I am part of the working class.

The struggling class.

The dreaming class.

The people who are the ones who truly make this world stand.

I'm just an ordinary woman.

So when I dream my dreams I feel this voice that tells me that once an ordinary girl always an ordinary girl. Great things couldn't happen to someone like me. And here's the fact: when you are an ordinary person everyone always reminds you everyday that you live you couldn't become what you dreamed. They tell you money matters, looks matter, and you should get a job that pays well. Life's hard. Little girls should try to find a doctor to marry because that's the only way you'll make it. That's the only way you'll grow up to be a somebody.

I stand on the street,

This ordinary girl that I am,

And no one notices or cares.

Because I get lost in the sea,

Of all the ordinary people.

Reasons, everyone always wants reasons why I am the way I am. Honestly, I would like to know myself. So I write about what hurts, what feels good, what makes me cry and what makes me feel. I want to know why:

I cry.

I'm screaming silently inside.

I'm happy for a moment and then I lose it.

I'm free but I hold back.

I hate myself every time I look in the mirror.

I drown in my self-pity.

I eat a tub of ice cream, then feel so much guilt that I can't move.

I am ashamed.

I hide from everything.

I feel more than I can take.

And I just really want to know why I am unable to be whole. Was I born with a failure inside of me that doesn't allow me to change? I spend my days scared. What if I never change? What if there are no reasons at all? What if I am the way I am forever and there is nothing I can do about it. So I look for an answer to make the confusion go away. Everyday I wake up searching with only the hope that someday something will be found that will make this endless longing go away.

Have you ever wanted something so bad you couldn't breathe?

I can't breathe.

Despair, I wanted to tell you a little bit about despair. Despair consumes me sometimes and takes me over. I've never been in the driver seat of my own self, it's always been my despair.

I regret so much about my life. I regret the things I didn't do. I regret the things that I forgot to do. I regret the things I was suppose to do and the things I did do. I regret until there is nothing left and I am simply nothing myself. I feel like I've already blown it sometimes. I feel like I have lost everything because I was scared. And that's what I regret most of all, all the fears.

I long to change it all and start over again. Take the steering wheel in my hands and put my life on to a new road.

To find my life without regrets and without my despair.

To find myself alive for the first time in my life.

The problem with everyone in this world is that they never take the time to breathe. They never take the time to let go. They never take the time to think about life. Hiding always from the real truth.

Always lost in despair.

Never looking to the sky.

Always to the ground.

The problem with everyone in this world is that they never forgive anyone. They never say they're sorry. They never let go of the pain that holds them. Assuming it's everybody else's fault.

They want the world to change around them.

Everyone is screaming inside.

Everyone is trying to figure it out.

Everyone is falling down.

Everyone is crying out.

I cry out to you across the valley.

Why don't you answer me?

I cry for my family because they don't cry for themselves.

Courage is my mother because she watched her own father die of cancer in a hospital. She was with him as he let go. How did it feel for her to watch part of her heart die with her father? She is the person I most want to be proud of me.

Strength is my father because he grew up in a house with eleven brothers and sisters. He didn't have a lot of things, but he took what he had and put himself through college. He is the most humble man I know. He is the person I most want to be like when I grow.

My parents, the people in this world who brought me here. I look at them, I really look at them.

They always remind me that life is hard. Life is rough, so I shouldn't dream so much because there is a chance that I could get let down.

I wonder, did they get let down in life? And I look at them, I really look at them.

Do they have any dreams anymore? Or is that something you lose when you get older?

I see the bills and the stresses over my brother and I. I see the stressful and annoying jobs they have to keep just to stay ahead.

But who are these people? These people I have known my whole life and yet don't know at all.

I would like to write the story of their lives so I could know every detail there ever was about them. I would like to change the world so they had no worries, no jobs, and no stresses.

They could have dreams again.

They are average people, but they show me everyday that average people are the greatest people to know.

Find myself to the point of breaking down again.

Lost and alone again.

The confusion makes me angry.

Tired of feeling this way.

You should see the way he holds her.

He really honestly loves her.

I am alone and always insecure.

Always trying to be something I'm not.

So sick of it.

We had a conversation about when I was younger.

Mom swears she should have held me back.

I was never a good reader.

Guess what?

I'm still not.

I was a dreamer back then.

Guess what?

I still am.

I guess some things never change.

I know that now.

I'm still here. I'm still lost. I'm still scared. My ass is still fat, terrorists still want to blow us up, and he still loves her. Does anyone have this secret place in their mind that they have created, hoping one day they'll see it?

I do, and I spend my nights creating each detail.

It's by the ocean.

I am on the sand.

The water touches my feet and then gently moves away.

I wish I could float away in the waves.

I wish I could fly away like the birds that circle above my head as I stand on that shore.

I am just thinking.

I am alone, but it is a good type of alone, because I am lost in the most beautiful moment I have ever been in. I finally find the answers to my questions in the waves, and I find peace in the colors of the sunset. It's a perfect place. A place where things are okay. I'm okay. Things change and I find happiness in the sand. The terrorists want to blow themselves up, and I have the power to make him love me more than life itself.

I am alive and free.

I am whole.

And I write about not the bad things but instead the joyful things I find in life. I write about the ocean and the sunsets. I write about the wind on my face and the sand that fills the spaces between my toes.

I feel so good,

On this little place by the ocean.

A place that only exists in my mind.

But I swear it's out there,

And someday that's where you'll find me.

But for now I am here just thinking, "Here am I, here is my life."

Late afternoon,

Inside my lonely room,

Examining the contents of my thighs.

I hate them so,

Because they are so fucking fat no matter which angle I look from.

I tear off my clothes,

And trace every piece of skin.

I am so imperfect.

Like an abstract painting waiting to be criticized.

Got this massive cottage ass,

I swear no treadmill could get rid of it.

The truth lies inside of my head,

When I say, "Who's going to love me this way?"

I could never get the good looking guys.

No one could desire me.

I certainly could not make it on looks alone.

I'm insecure and shy.

What am I going to do,

To feel safe in a group of good looking women?

I read thirty pages on the internet about how to make my skin smoother.

No luck. Tough luck.

"Girl, you should love what the lord gave to you."

I wish I was taller, my thighs smaller, my skin smoother, my breasts fuller, my nose thinner, and my hair shiner.

I wish I was happy.

Pick up a magazine and look at a girl who stole the body that I was suppose to have.

Oh, fuck it.

Who needs feelings anyway when you can feel numb?

I get depressed and eat like a hog. Then I get depressed again and the
treadmill calls so I'm on it.

I run,

Until I am sure I won't be able to feel anything in the morning.

My body hurts,

And I hurt.

I wish I were one of those strong women who don't exercise and like their
bodies just as they are.

I go to the bathroom and look at the mirror.

I touch my fingers to the glass where my reflection is.

Holy God, that's me.

The reflection of this girl.

You should see this girl.

And when you do, tell her she's okay,

She never listens to me.

It was summer when two girls rode on a boat in a lake. The next day one girl came up to me and said,

"The other girl thinks your fat."

And I fell spectacularly apart because it was the moment. The moment I lost it. When that girl told me of what the other girl had said I fell into the waves of self-abuse.

I was in sixth grade. Suddenly, I wanted to go on a diet. I wanted to get a treadmill. I started to read food labels. I was fat, it had been confirmed. I knew it already, but because someone else had said it,

I lost it.

I was so young to lose my self worth, but I let it all go anyway and till this day I can't believe one little girl's words could affect me so much.

So much destruction occurred.

So much pain was built.

I am what I am because of that one moment.

I hurt just the same. I look in the mirror and feel the same way as I did back then as though nothing ever changes.

I am fat.

And everyday I get into my own boat,

And drift out, thinking about all the times when I was okay.

Okay with me.

But then I sink into that familiar sea.

The sea of doubts and fears. The sea that whispers that I am not okay and I never will be until I prove that little girl wrong.

Till I stop hurting.

And everyday is a battle.

All because of a day in summer a long time ago,

When two little girls rode on a boat in a lake.

Cold water surrounds my empty body.

God, I am drowning.

I am lost so deep in this cold water.

They wrap their arms tight around me, enclosing me.

They press their lips against my skin.

They whisper their love.

They swear they understand me.

They know me.

"Why are you so sad, Colleen?" They whisper against my ear.

I don't know how to respond, so I don't.

But all my life,

I wish I could say,

"You wonder why I have built all these walls, don't you remember
you're the one who helped me put them up?"

I think that now I understand that no one knows me and I know no one.

I think sometimes I just want everyone to get off of me.

Away from me.

They are always so certain that they got me all figured out.

They think they can help me and then use me.

I just want them to leave sometimes.

Just leave,

You remind me of everything I don't want to be anymore.

Fat girl,

Wanders around the world,

Wearing a fake smile,

Saying, "I like myself this way."

Fat girl,

All her friends say she looks great.

Nobody knows,

The absolute hate she has for herself.

Fat girl,

Watching all the skinny girls,

All the skinny girls who shine.

She looks at herself in the mirror.

Fat girl,

Sighs every time she weighs herself.

She sees her reflection.

She sees a monster.

Fat girl,

Wants to disappear sometimes.

She wants anything but this.

She has dreams at night.

Fat girl is a liar.

Fat girl is me.

I always sigh at the girls who throw up in the toilets but secretly I think I
could go that far myself.

Just to lose a little weight.

But I think what sets me apart from those girls and keeps me from losing it,
is that I realize that it's not just about the weight. Even if I lost a hundred
pounds I still wouldn't be okay. I'd still be missing something.

I started another diet this week,

But I broke it and ate chocolate today.

Actually I ate so much chocolate,

It really is a wonder why I didn't just shit out whole bricks of it.

It's a wonder,

But life is a wonder.

I think dieting makes me nuts.

Swirling and spinning, I lay on the ground looking at all the people who stand above me.

I've fought so hard and lost so well. I want to stand on top and look at all that are below me and laugh.

But on my way I was knocked off.

So I lay on the ground.

I scream in frustration but nobody hears me.

I'm not good enough for anyone.
I'm not good enough for anything.

I want to be writer. I want to be a good writer. But all I see when I write is meaningless. I'm meaningless. I have no purpose here, I am just simply an extra. I swear that I am bursting with emotions that I know if only someone could understand them then they would think I'm great. But my writings are shit, and I'm jealous of people with real talents. I want to be a writer. I wanted to tell you the truth and be great. I don't want to wait forever until someone notices that I'm alive.

But my soul is screaming every time that I try.

I'm not good enough for anyone.
I'm not good enough for anything.

Driving in the yellow taxi, picking up my baggage and bullshit for the day, I come across you standing there along side of the road. I pass you by, but my mind says I should turn around.

But not to pick you up to give you a ride.

To run your ass over,

Back up,

And run your ass over again.

Simple hours. Slow hours. Long hours. Hours that tick like a minute hand in my mind. I am a high school student living in a high school world.

Head on my desk, I spend my hours dreaming.

I dream about a day when I am free of this meaningless babble they speak to me. I dream of the day when they will call me an adult and actually respect my thoughts and ideas. I dream that I will see all the things they only told me about.

I am bursting,

With dreams of the way things are going to be when I get out of here.

I am a dreamer,

Lost in the thoughts of my head. I look out the window and see the world. It smiles and beckons to me.

"Come see for yourself."

But I am lost in these simple hours. Slow hours. Very long hours. Stuffed up in a room with thirty other people,

All dreaming.

Somehow I think that all these hours will add up to days. Days when I could have been living a new life. Days when I could be driving away with the wind in my hair. Days when I forgot about who I once was and got lost in who I was becoming.

Days when I actually felt alive.

It's just that it's so hard to tell in this cave of a room they put you in if there's a world out there. The teacher has passed out the test and I almost certainly will fail. I look at the girl next to me and she begins to fill out the answers with confidence.

She will grow up to be a scholar.

My main goal in life is to learn to waltz.

I will fail in school.

24

Infact, I think my presence in high school can be compared to a tile on the floor of an Arby's bathroom.

I was nothing in high school.

I look out the window again and I find that it's raining. I imagine myself dancing in the downpour.

I will fail in school.

But in terms of life,

That is where I will succeed.

I will live a life that is alive and it will be my own.

In life, I will be everything I spent hours dreaming myself to be in high school.

When there is a man drifting out to sea in the fog, there is always a girl standing at the shore waving good-bye.

It was a simple time in my life and he was just one simple man that entered my life for only a short while. Glen Moore, a man that you never knew and one I barely knew myself. He was my mother's father, making him my grandpa. I don't know much about him. The sorrow is thick when my family talks about him, so we rarely have discussions. I don't remember much about him either.

Do you know that I can see his face sometimes?
I don't know why I think about him so much because I was so young when he died. I don't remember a lot about him. My family tells stories of this man who holds me in his arms in pictures of me when I was a baby. I see a man that I don't know now, but something in my body realizes that I did know him at one point. I think I must have loved him beyond words. Though I can't remember a lot about him, I have a few vague memories. I remember him in his room in the hospital. My mom had to beg the nurse to let my brother and I up to see him, and I remember walking into the room and seeing his face. I can see his face even now as I am writing this. The bed was on the left, one single bed, and there he was looking at me. It was the last time I would ever get to see him. I wish now that I said so much more than I did then. But I didn't understand. I didn't realize that he was leaving us.
I remember everyone crying back at my grandma's house after he had died. I was so proud of myself because I was not crying. I was the only one who wasn't crying, but I suppose this was because I had no idea what I had lost.

He was gone,

And I didn't even really have a chance to say good-bye. Not the right way, not the way good-byes should be. All I had left was pictures of him and I, and the stories that they tell me. The stories I can't even remember.

The only other memory I have of my grandpa was when he was fishing on a dock in Petoskey. My brother and I walked up behind him and scared him. I remember there was an old fishing pole in the water below us. I have walked those docks many times hoping by some chance I would find that fishing pole so I would know the exact place my grandpa stood, but I have not found it. Do you know that I can feel him around me? I can feel him near me now reading everything that I write.

I read one of my mother's college papers about his death. She was there in the hospital room when he passed on. She wrote that just before he died he called out her name. What did he want to say? I don't mean to be selfish in this way, but I always wondered if he wanted to say something to me. Did I cross his mind as he left? What do people think about when they die?

Do you want to know the strangest thing about it all?

I honestly miss him.

I miss him so much that I ache. How is it possible for me to miss someone so much when I have exactly two memories of them when they were alive? I think, maybe, I might have loved him endlessly, because something is still connected between him and I even today. The emotions of the little girl that I once was still exists. So it would be the greatest gift to talk to him again. I can see his face because we have pictures, but what did he smell like? What did his voice sound like?

27

I miss it.

There is something missing inside of me just because of the simple fact that he's not here with me, and because I never got the chance to really know him.

He used to love to fish when he was alive. I love to fish now but I have no one to take me. I bet he would have taken me if he were still around. And if I could create a moment in my life that never really took place it would be of us fishing on a lake. Me as I am now and him as he was back then. I think we would have talked about everything.

But he's gone.

It leaves you with a hole in your life, because you never got to say good-bye.

I suppose he will forever be drawn in my mind as the greatest man I once knew but didn't really know at all. My two memories are small but I'll take them, because that is the only thing I have besides the left over feelings inside of my body. I wish I could see him again so much that I ache. He used to call me "squirt". He was the only person in my life to give me a nickname. I wonder if I ever saw him would he call me that again as though nothing had changed since he left. I cry sometimes over the fact that he's gone. He left a hole inside of me. I never got a real chance with him, you know? It's beautifully sad.

But he's gone.

I feel him around me and I know he's here, I really honestly do. My favorite picture of him and I was when I was just a baby and I was sitting in his lap. He was looking down at me and I was wearing a sombrero.

I miss him.

Everyone is losing, until one day they themselves are lost. It is the human pattern.

In my dreams,

We walked together.

It was cloudy,

We talked forever.

It felt good to be by you once again.

Do you know it now because I never had the chance to tell you then?

Did I forget to say it?

I just wanted you to know,

I'll love you forever,

So it's okay that you have to go.

Written on February 21, 2003 at 12:05 A.M, on my bed, staring at the ceiling of my room. Where were you at this moment?

I am here.

The place I have always found myself to be.

I was pacing in my room just minutes ago,

Dreaming myself a thousand times around this world to other places.

There is a silence.

I speak no words of how I feel.

I only write.

Write until I cry.

Write until I am too tired to think.

It's the only way I feel whole anymore.

The wind is smashing against the window, waking everything but my soul.

Do you think there is something out there beyond that glass window?

I've dreamt about it.

Do you think there is something more inside of me than all this pain?

Do you think I can rise above it all?

Sometimes I wish so much it hurts.

I saw the stars out from my front yard this night.

They were just one other thing in this world that I will never touch.

I watched one fall down to the earth in a streak of light.

I wanted to pick that falling star back up and put it back in the sky,

But I could not fix it.

Sometimes I feel a distance from my own self.

Like a star from the night,

I fall.

Like a human from the earth,

31

I watch and make a wish for a change in my life.

And I wonder,

At that moment was anyone looking to the sky and wondering the same?

Did they feel it too?

And I think, well I think, maybe in the end I'm just a little scared.

What if I can't be fixed just like that star?

What if I can never rise again after my fall?

But now,

I am just alone in my room.

I stare at my ceiling,

Just thinking,

Always thinking.

Do you ever notice the pain that attached itself to your life? It's not strong or easy to see, but it is always lingering inside the deep walls. And you keep it well hidden.

I know that it exists in everyone and everyday it is the one thing that remains the same. The variable that you can compare to, whether it's higher, lower, or just the same.

I am not saying that people are doomed to agony in this life but I know now for certain that this is all true. There is a sadness to life and everyone is and should be able to feel it freely. Examine it fully, because it means that you have lived.

Everyone runs away from this sadness, so do I. I think I run and hide from it all because I am afraid that if I acknowledge my pain, my sadness, the world will turn on me. The people will walk away and I will be unable to be loved. For this place had told us the only thing can be at all times is happy.

Happiness should always be sought and I do believe it can be found, but realize the sadness. Realize the joy because you have lived and also lost.

I know this goes against the grain of the world but I am saying that it's okay. It's okay to feel a little pain, even when everything in the world is great. The sadness is not a disease, instead, it proves that you have lived and as you lived you have felt.

Went to another graduation party and felt low. God, I really hate graduation parties. I never feel alive. I never feel right. I don't ever to seem to quite fit in anywhere in the group. I spend most of my time avoiding people and searching for all the men I am in love with. I didn't bring my bathing suit even though the water on the lake looked inviting. My insecurities got the best of me again.

My parents don't want me to talk back. "I'm your mother/father, that's why!" They don't understand that I have to. My whole life I have never said anything and lately I feel like I'm going to self-combust.

I left the party with my parents and went home.

And I sat there on my bed,

And just thought about things for a while.

Where's my joy?

How can I show these people how great I am,

When I can't even break down this wall?

I wanted them to look at me and see,

Something different from what they saw before.

All I have ever wanted,

In this whole world,

Was for them,

To see me,

Shining,

For them.

Just one time,

I wanted them to wonder about who I really am.

I have never been part of the social scene, never knew the right things to say. Lost always in the fact that I am not noticed.

No one cares or wants to know about Colleen.

So she just sits there quietly.

Slowly sipping on her milk, so she sits.

I am just an intellectual, this is the reason I am quiet and always left to observe. I am just an individual, I certainly don't need anyone.

But no one notices me. I am translucent in this world. I have never been special, never been worth it.

Everything feels rather cold and I spend my time thinking about it.

The girls trying to impress the boys.

The boys trying to impress the girls.

And me, somewhere painfully out of place and in between.

The social conversation. The laughter. The heat that rises, and someone is making another person love them by their words.

That is what I lack,

The words to make them love me.

The moment when I say the right thing to make everyone love me.

Sometimes, I suppose, I feel rather left out. Rather different. Rather unappreciated.

And I always wondered why?

I am a good girl.

Sometimes I think about doing very bad things.

Sometimes,

I want to get drunk until I can't feel my body.

I want to shoot drugs into my arms until I can fly.

I want to flunk out.

I want to ruin everything that I have.

I want to find a guy and let him take me for all I'm worth.

I want to smoke a cigarette and get addicted.

I want to not eat until I'm skin and bones.

I want to get into fights just so I can make someone scream.

But there is something inside of me that says,

"You're too good for that.

You're a good girl.

You're a virgin.

You've never seen pot nor you don't like the smell of smoke.

You're a puppet.

You never lose control of yourself.

You always have everything in your hand.

You pray to God every night."

Sometimes I feel like I want to lose control and find myself on the ground.

Sometimes I want to do bad things, very bad things.

Good girls are invisible.

They are not noticed because they keep it hidden and under control.

But you should know,

Good girls,

Always have the worst thoughts.

Sometimes,

I want to break out and tear this world and myself apart and leave you all
wondering.

Let it all go to hell.

Be a very bad girl.

I have to go pray to God now.

Ask him to forgive me for all the very bad thoughts I have.

Like all the other invisible good girls.

I live my life for you, just so you know. I find myself constantly and always thinking,

What will my family think?

What will my friends say?

Who in this world will back me up?

No one.

And because I live my life for everyone but myself, once one disapproving eye turns my way,

I'm out.

I back away.

Just to keep the peace.

It's ironic you know.

Sometimes I think I can be selfish about some things, but it turns out my life is a course someone else planned for me.

I really have no control.

Let's face it,

Most of the greatest battles were fought alone.

But how?

How can I stand in a crowd of peers and stand alone?

To finally look them in the eye and say, "No, that is not what I want."

To have the strength.

To take control.

To take the steering wheel.

Push everyone aside and finally listen,

To my heart,

That beats out a pattern that tells me the truth.

To my soul,

That shows me what I really want.

To my destiny,

That tells me that I'm going the wrong way.

I go the wrong way because of you.

I want so much,

For you just to be happy with me.

But I don't think I can do this anymore.

Where does this endless shit come from?

I am always at a lost for how much I can gather within.

I am like a packrat to my soul.

Placing and putting, shoving it all so it will look clean for when guests arrive. To hire a maid in my soul would be like asking for help. This is a distance in my life I will not nor will ever go.

It all goes to the same place, the heart.

And it flows outward to the soul and beyond.

And I really have no room for anymore shit.

Maybe they're right about me. Maybe they were always right from the very beginning. You see, all my life I have had these great fears about everything I do. I get scared so easily and I freeze up. All my life, believe it or not, I have wanted to be an actress. Just like my dreams of becoming a writer, I wanted to expose and express myself to people. With acting there was a face behind the words. People could see the emotions. I used to tell people this all the time, but now I am ashamed. The way they looked at me when I did tell them made me stop. They couldn't ever picture me as an actress. I am shy, timid at times, insecure, and I suppose very non-actress like. I can't even talk in front of ten people without breaking into a sweat. Every time now I speak about it, I even can't believe myself. I guess when people bring you down enough you start to believe the things they say. But what do you do with left over dreams when they are secretly the one thing you desire the most?

Like I have said before, I wanted to tell you the truth. I wanted to say all the things I never got to say. I wanted to scream, cry, and laugh. I wanted to perfect the art of it all. I wanted to break my shell and I wanted everyone to see it. I wanted to make you weep and understand.

But I can't image myself trying it. Flying out to Los Angeles, going to auditions, living in a cheap place, barely scraping by. How can people do that anyway? It takes strength, but it makes me scared.

But I dream of it,

And I never speak of it.

Sometimes I know that I am capable of being strong. Sometimes I know that I can achieve anything. I know that I can make it in any situation, but something inside stops me. And I don't know how to break down that wall. How can I prove to myself that I shouldn't be scared when I am too scared to even try? When everyone around me tells me no?

You see, all my life I have wanted to travel the world. I want to go to different places and find the pieces that have been missing in my life. But I want to do it alone. No friends or family. Just me,

Only me.

But I can't imagine myself going on planes, hailing taxes, trying to speak different languages, when I am alone. I can't do it alone because I am too scared.

Do you know how badly I have wanted to do it alone? Stand on top of my fears and know that I did it all by myself. Do you know I keep a packet of places I would like to go in my room? I try to find out all the information I would need to do it alone,

But I don't think I ever would.

And even though I say I want to write, if I were to ever publish this, I would be terrified because there is always that chance that someone could just turn away.

I have always thought people have second guessed me, but now I realized that maybe they are right on about me. They say I can't be an actress let alone a writer. They say I will never travel alone, and I will never find a way out of this fear.

Maybe they have it right.

Maybe this is who I am and I have no chance in hell of becoming the girl I dreamed of in my head.

And now I get it.

Now I understand why people act the way they do.

Why people stay in the same place all their lives.

Why people don't get out of abusive relationships.

Why people stay in jobs they hate for thirty years of their lives.

Why races rarely marry or date outside to other races.

Why I haven't told anyone the truth.

Because everyone is too scared.

Scared of the failure.

The ideas people would have.

People talking about us or simply disliking us.

The idea of change.

Finally telling the truth about ourselves.

Doing something that could be hard instead of easy.

Leaving our safe zone.

Just taking the chance that everything could go wrong and the whole world would be against us.

I want to buy this painting someday of this woman and a man who are dancing in the rain.

I secretly want to be that woman.

But you know what? I couldn't do that in my lifetime. I could never dance in the rain. Because people don't do that here anymore and I don't have the strength to be different. I can never really be that free.

I freeze up every time.

Now I have realized that my life is nothing, it doesn't matter. Because I have allowed myself to fall off track because I am too scared to take the chances. I am too scared to fight for what I truly want.

Sometimes I want to be free of myself so I can become someone completely different. I would want to become someone who has strength and courage and dances in the rain.

She takes her life and lives out her dreams because she is fearless.

She is an actress who travels the world,

And does it alone.

She is fearless.

I want to be free so much of these chains I create for myself. I want to break down the mold that everyone has created for me,

But I can't.

I don't know how and these fears hold me back from trying.

And it hurts every night when I go to sleep because I know I'll dream of this life that I don't know if I ever will lead.

And I can't fight for it.

But I want to fight for it so bad.

I wish for strength sometimes, because I don't want them to be right about me.

They can't be right.

I sit in the dim and remember that one time when I was so young to lose touch of myself. I think I was in fourth grade when it happened. I remember I was friends with this blonde haired girl who was always in trouble. To me she was everything that was free and I wished I could be her. I think I have spent my life wishing to be free but when I was younger I didn't understand the emotions I was feeling.

That girl and I used to talk on the phone together for hours and we used to make up stories about how we were going to run away and become movie stars. When my mother overheard the conversation and confronted me, I cried and said it was truth. I think somewhere in my body I wanted to run away, it wasn't just a fantasy. So I was mortified that no one would love me because of this. Had I betrayed everyone around me for secretly wishing to abandon them and everything I had?

Slowly, I wasn't able to be friends with the little blonde haired girl anymore, and the world knew about the situation before I knew what was happening myself. I was ashamed because it was true. So I hid from everyone and found myself locked against my sadness because it felt as though no one would forgive me. How could they forgive when it was what I truly wanted?

Isolation filled me and I spend that year feeling overwhelmed. I remember wishing someone would tell me I was okay. When I awoke from that dark point in my life, I realized I had been left behind. One way to describe it was, it was this great race and I fell. When I finally got up, I was so far behind that no matter how fast I ran I couldn't catch up to everyone else. Years and days have past since that time and I still want people to tell me I'm okay. I still feel overwhelmed and left behind. I still want to run away. I still want to be free.

How can I be free?

I can't see what is beyond these walls.

As I stand next to you, why can't you see I am not really here at all?

The show is over so take a bow.

Do you mean anything you ever said to anyone?

You put on your copper mask and hide the pain.

You tell me what to do but you don't even know what to do yourself.

You're lost,

But you never show it.

You're scared,

But no one could ever guess it about you.

Every man for himself.

Everyone hides from the truth.

No one is who they really are.

And I hate it all so much.

Everything brakes around me.

Everyone tears me apart.

I used to care.

I used to have compassion and trust,

But you tore it away.

Now I put on my copper mask and stand next to you on that stage.

The show must go on,

But I wanted you to know that you all are a bunch of fucking liars.

I saved a cockroach from the floor of Glen's. I didn't want to do it but you should have seen the way it looked at me. Suddenly, I couldn't turn away. I watched it twist and turn on it's black back. A woman next to me saw it and looked away in absolute disgust. I tried to concentrate on something else. I read the labels on the cans of food. My eyes wandered back to that cockroach. It twisted and turned on that hard floor all because it just wanted to live. People moved passed and paid no attention.

I couldn't help it.

I grabbed a piece of a paper bag and picked the cockroach up. The man at the checkout asked me if everything was okay. I said yes. I left with that cockroach still in my hand.

Out of the corner of my eye, I saw the woman who was standing next to me shaking her head in disgust.

I got in my car,

I drove to a nearby ATM machine where there was these yellow flowers. I put the cockroach by the one with the nicest blooms.

I hope that cockroach is alive and well today.

You know what?

I think I care too much,

And I think in life I'm going to get walked over.

Isn't that what happens to people who care too much?

But I wanted that cockroach to live,

Because I also wish to live.

I am not a Catholic, but it is what I have been labeled since the day I was born, so that is what I always said I was.

But, honestly, I know I'm really not.

I find myself believing in other things. I find pieces of me in other religions and other cultures.

But what am I if I am not a Catholic?

It is what I was given since the day I was born. It was my label. Everyone in this world needs a label attached to them.

So when they asked, I said, "I'm a Catholic." I sang in the choir and said all the prayers.

I was lying,

Because even as I responded to the prayers and I sang every song I did not believe a word.

He knows too.

He can listen to my heart,

And I lied.

Everyone wants you to choose a religion. And once you choose, you have to follow the rules. You have to choose one religion, and when you do you have to fight for it against all other religions.

But I find that I am not on anyone's side. I suppose in a way I don't feel like I have the power in me to believe in one religion because I honestly don't believe in one religion fully.

I am not a Catholic,

But I am nothing else either.

I believe in a higher being and that is all I know for sure. All other stories and religious beliefs, I don't know. I only know that there is someone or something greater out there watching us and protecting us. And I think religions are all just the same, because in the end, we connect into one world of believers.

Every night I pray.

I pray for peace in the world and peace of mind.

I pray for love and a space in this world that is solely mine.

I am not a Catholic,

But I am nothing else either.

I am simply nothing at all.

I woke up today to find it was Lent. Lent, another pointless religious time in my life. Priests tell me if I give up something for forty days that I will be enlightened with the spirit of God. Everyone around me gives up meat, ice cream, sanity, boys, chewing their nails, and so on...

I stand there and try.

But in the end, I feel nothing, nothing at all. And after forty days of trying and failing, I am nothing. I would like to know what I need to do to make myself whole. Because God knows, I think I would do just about anything to feel good again.

And so today when the phone rang and my father said, "Quick Colleen, it might be God." I ran like hell, because maybe he had something good to say.

"I don't think you want to be around people, Colleen. I really don't think you do." I knew that from the first moment it was said that it was true, but I knew that it wasn't also right. I want to be around people, I really do. I want people to want to be around me. It's just that every now and then I get sick of everyone and their bullshit. Sometimes I feel completely vulnerable to everything. I feel weak and out of place, and I don't want to let people into me. I guard myself. I do this because of so many reasons that I can't think of one. I just feel like I don't want to get hurt. I don't like the sound of trust when it brakes. But I do like human beings, even if they make me feel lonelier than hell. I guess maybe I'm just hiding for a while. But I do not want to be alone for the rest of my life. Please note: I don't want to be alone for the rest of my life.

I build my walls ten feet high.

I never let anyone come through,

So no wonder no one knows.

I guard my gates with a hundred soldiers.

No one can come in.

I am always ready for an attack,

Even if one may never come.

I look to the gray drenched sky above me.

I will never let you in.

I will never fall in love wholely,

Because I build my walls ten feet high.

You let me down again but it's okay.

I realize I have no real friends anyway.

Every time I think I won't get hurt someone hurts me.

Today it was you.

It wasn't a big shock, I figure by the time I die everyone in this world will have had a turn at me and will have hurt me in some way or another.

So today it was you.

You hurt me deeply but it's okay.

I realize that no one likes me anyway.

Everyone invests so much time in their life tearing everyone apart around them and it's never going to change.

Today you tore at my skin and now I bleed.

You made me bleed so you laugh because it gives you strength.

And it's okay.

I'm not worth it anyway.

I lay on the ground thinking of you.

I'll put myself back together till the next time I fall from the pain that someone else's heart has afflicted on me.

I cry because today it was you,

And I wanted to pretend that you would never hurt me.

But you did, so I lay and try to understand.

You wouldn't believe the unbelievable amounts of sorrow you can feel when you wake up every morning and feel dead. Just like a corpse that breathes. I swear to myself every night that this time things are going to be different and things will change.

I will wake up,

And for once in my life,

I will feel alive.

Do I have what it takes to finally be satisfied with life? I want to take on another day and not have that overwhelming urge to run away. When that doesn't happen everyday I feel so much. So many emotions that all I can feel is the numbness that circles through my body. I can't comprehend much anymore. It's like someone took all my strength and fight out of me.

I try, God, I really try.

I want to change and find my way through this, whatever this may be. I whisper encourages to myself every night.

I wish endlessly about so much. Do you?

Everyday I wake up to wish for a better tomorrow. Everyday I wake up hoping to forget yesterday. Everyday I feel this deep sorrow that eats away everything that's good inside of me. Everyday I fade into the invisible air around me.

In my head,

Thinking tomorrow,

Maybe tomorrow.

Colleen Cherwinski.

What a simple odd name.

Nothing particular about it that's worth anything to anyone.

Colleen Nicole Cherwinski.

I wonder if I'll be remembered after all is said and done?

Will Colleen Cherwinski ring out for years to come?

But what has my life done,

That would be worth remembering?

I am nothing.

Just a nobody standing alone.

Why don't you see?

The reason I try so hard not to be ordinary,

Is because I don't want to be forgotten.

I don't want to be nothing.

I want to be more than just Colleen Cherwinski.

I'll be around for much longer,

If I could be something more.

I had a dream the other day as I laid outside,

That I could be a somebody.

Plain as I am,

I have this determination that I think everyone underestimates.

I won't stop trying.

I won't stop dreaming.

Most dream me to be a teacher with a truckload of children in my minivan.

I am so far from that.

I dream myself too far to stop here.

And I dream every day to every night that I am somebody.

Colleen Cherwinski is a somebody.

57

Everything falls like rain on my best days.

The sky shatters, my mind bends and brakes to reveal I have no intelligence.

No beauty.

The night is like a dark drink and I always thought if I had the chance I would shallow it whole.

Then the light would radiant through me, hitting your eyes.

Hit you, and the rain would flow inside my thirsty body.

If this happened I would be special.

The girl who swallowed the moon.

Drunk on the stars,

But still fell like rain.

If you were to fall from the sky right now and jump into a scene of my life, here is how it would go:

There I was in Little Caesar's with a group of friends from my drama group. It's funny I can even call them friends because as I sat there I felt lonely as hell. I said things that I didn't mean just so I could have something to talk about. I pretended once again I was someone I wasn't. Everything should have been fine, and yet, it wasn't at all. Why was I so depressed? I found myself looking out the window, drowning out the conversation around me, and wondering: If you turned the world over from the exact point where I was sitting, where in the world would it land on? And for God's sake, would I be happier there than I am now? Could I find some peace of mind there?

Do you ever feel insignificant?

Ever feel little?

Like people could walk right through you?

No one notices you're alive.

You sit down and try to remember the best time in your life.

You can't remember a moment at all.

You feel your heart ache.

Something brakes in the deep caves of you.

You can't describe it all,

So you never say a word.

But you feel like an earthquake inside.

You feel something that doesn't have a name.

You think, "If only the world could crawl inside my body, then they would
see how great I am."

Then they would see you standing there.

Quiet,

But so very loud all the same.

Everyone around you has it figured out.

Your soul screams for a happiness that you have never known.

A happiness that you try desperately everyday to find.

You would give just about anything for a chance to change your life.

You would give anything for the strength to feel.

Yeah,

Sometimes I feel like that too.

There was a big party and I swear everyone I knew went to it.

I wanted to go, but a voice inside my head said, "Just drive on Colleen."

So I did.

I drove past the house.

I speed down the black top and rolled down my window.

Through the windshield of my car,

I saw how bright the sky can be even in the middle of the night.

I brushed the hair from my face and turned on the radio.

I just drove on.

There was this big party,

I still don't really know why I didn't go.

I think about leaving so much that sometimes I wonder if I am going to miss anything. I sat with my family for a Sunday dinner. I looked and I saw all their faces. Their wonderful faces that I would do anything for. And as we talked, I realized that if I left we wouldn't ever have those family Sunday dinners.

I really love those dinners.

And I thought about how everything was going to change and then I got scared. I realized that when I do leave, I am going to miss the little things. My trees in my backyard, the air around here, the faces that I knew, the way I could walk around with no shoes on, and my safe haven.

I feel it slipping through my fingers.

Who's going to eat dinner with me when I do leave? Where am I going? Am I going to be alone forever? To tell you the honest truth, I feel like I'm breaking something.

Will that be me someday?

The lonely stranger in the café,

Who sits all alone,

Thinking helplessly of those Sunday dinners I once knew.

The news keeps saying that the economy is down.

Slowly declining and everyone falls.

People losing their homes and jobs.

Mom and Dad trying to figure out exactly how broke we are and how we are going to get through it all.

We just finished a great war.

Terrorists still want to kill us all anyway.

Love is on the decline too.

Economists say buy more.

Commercials of hungry children, lonely children, fatherless children.

But at least we won the Goddamn war.

I hope in heaven there are bars and everyone can smoke a joint without any worry of dying. It won't matter who you are.

There's too much dying here,

Bodies and souls.

All the religious say to love one another.

Just a few restrictions:

Do not have an abortion.

Do not love a different race.

Find one religion, then find a way to kill all other religions.

Find who you are, and when you do change for me.

Do not fall in love with the same sex.

Start wars in the name of your God because that will solve everything, not to mention give you a straight passageway to heaven.

Condemn everyone around you, even though you do the same.

If you don't follow these rules, we'll come and string you up like a dead rabbit.

Compassion is dying too.

The only way you really feel it is if you pay $7.50 to see a movie where a white woman falls in love with a black man and in the end the world finally accepts them.

The world never changes.

People have tried to change the world.

Poets, philosophers, the religious,

But nothing is becoming,

Everything is because we make it that way.

We write about the fighters in our magazines and newspapers.

But we never join the crusade.

Where do you think this will lead?

Can you even imagine?

And everything fades away.

Just like me.

Just like you.

No matter what we did or who we were in life.

Where will the horses go when there is no more land for them to run free? When times change and the capacity of human life overcomes the world. When the air is too populated to breathe. When the nuclear bombs from that one great last war splits the earth in half, leaving something missing, and no more room for anything that takes up space. When there are hovercrafts and no need for cornfields and long dirt roads. There will be no use for the sun, moon, or the sky.

Because there wasn't any room after half the earth fell away, they came to one conclusion: soak up all the oceans and rivers that were left to make room for all the space age babies. All sea creatures died not because they had a choice, but because we felt like they had to.

There was no more room for the trees, birds, or flowers. All of nature's things could only be read about in books. Computer chips were placed in your head, but there were no more sunsets. Grass was only found in museums. It couldn't be bought, for the cost would be too great. Food is grown in tubes in factories.

There is no poetry or stories, because there is nothing beautiful anymore. Everyone has forgotten how to fall in love. Compassion is only a word in an old dictionary. And I wonder all the same, where will the horses go? There will be museums built for them. Large pictures of them running free on the plains. Pictures of the western and Native American people on their backs. Pictures of when they were our only way of seeing the world. Their eyes a glow and their body glistening, they were our companions. People were awed by their simple grace. There will be statues of them erected and children will ask their parents, but their parents will not know why. Where did the horses go? In a diary, a young girl will read of her ancestor's wild mustang. That little girl will never know what it felt like to feel a horse beneath her body. She will never feel the rock of a horse that roamed thousands of years before her.

When the last horse died, the world cried and built him a tomb of gold. His name was Fred and he used to give children rides on his back. They added the species to the extinct list, and soon it was followed by so many others.

In the end, there were no animals. No plants or other things,

Just humans and cement.

I look out my window and I see an open space. Trees and birds fill the earth and they surround me. They say civilization is on the rise and technology is the key. But do humans truly realize the power they have? The power they have to make or destroy something.

But where will the horses go?

When it comes down to the fact that only humans can be left. Once we destroy everything in our path with our wars and our constant need for growing and destruction there simply won't be any room,

For the horses,

The simple lovely horses.

I am so glad I won't be around to see it go. For now I have my trees, my fields, and my sunsets. They say that if you freeze your body you can live a long life and wake up thousands of years later. Please don't bring me back. I don't want to see. They say they will gain so much. I see the loss is so deep. No matter how much we try, humans are meant to fail. And someday it will be so great that the world will stop and cry.

And the world will know that there will be no place where the horses can go to be safe.

I stand outside and the gentle breeze hits my face. My hair flies and something speaks to me. My whole life I never thought I could save anything. I never thought I was really worth anything to anyone.

I never was the strong one.

Never the righteous one.

I never quite fit the mold of the next new age Mother Theresea. But I look around at this world and I see something that needs to be saved. I see the pain but I also see the glimpse of hope. I hear a call in the wind that comes towards me. At first I thought it would move right past me and to another person who was so much stronger than me, but the call stopped and flowed through me, it entered me.

Maybe I am somebody strong.

Maybe I can leave something behind when I'm gone.

Maybe my fears will fuel me to surpass all I ever dreamed myself to be.

Maybe I could be the one single person that changes everything.

So I asked God today if he wanted me to try to find a way to heal all the pain here in this place. I got no words, instead, I got a storm. Hail, freezing rain, ice, and snow all mixed together, coming down in April buckets. I have never gotten a sign from God before so I wasn't sure if it all was meant to answer me. Maybe I'm just being naïve and stupid, but I hear a knocking of wind on my window right now saying that maybe I should get up and do what my soul has been screaming for me to do for so long. Even if I am ordinary now maybe my life is meant to be something extraordinary.

Can it be possible?

Has a path revealed itself to me or am I just crazy?

I hear it again, calling me.

Does someone need me?

Excuse my hesitation but I don't think I have ever been needed before.

It's almost amazing to have something inside that is calling,

"Maybe you could Colleen,

Maybe you could."

Can I be honest? I don't think we're going to make it.

The human race, that is.

Everyone stands around and points fingers at each other even though it comes down to the simple fact that we don't understand each other. The races, the religious, the different classes, the ignorants, all get together in their own groups and start conspiracies. And it's all so ridiculous and so not worth the time, and yet, it is what we do best.

I'm sorry you don't feel understood. I'm sorry you feel we've populated the world with unholy ideas. I'm sorry that you think women shouldn't be heard and that being gay is wrong. I'm sorry that you think you're race is superior. I'm sorry if you don't like any religion but your own. I'm truly sorry,

But not at all.

Because don't you see we are all just the same. You sit around in your little bubble of a world and pick everyone around you apart, plotting destruction.

But every one of us is so wrong.

We are all unfair to one another. We all judge and prosecute. And don't deny it, because I can see your shortcomings from where I stand now. Can you see mine?

Would you like to see the scars on my heart? No, they wouldn't match yours but they are there still. Would you like to come to our home one day to see that we are not as bad as you once thought?

Don't you see it?

We're all dying. We're all suffering. It's not just one race, one gender, one religion, or one nation,

The whole world is dying.

The human race is dying.

Can't you see that or are you blind to it?

68

We're all dying.

We are all the same though we are all not alike. We are all flesh and bone. We are all driven by greed. We are all love and hatred. We are all what our mothers and fathers taught us to be.

We touch the same waters and ground. We breathe the same oxygen and stare at the same sky. We all live, die, and become the ground we walk on. We are all human beings, all descendents of one another. All related by blood.

And we're dying,

Because from the very first day we were put on this earth we have done nothing but cause destruction and fight one another. We start wars and tear each other apart until there is nothing left. We point fingers when the only people to blame is ourselves.

Don't you realize?

The fight is not with humans, instead, it is within humans.

And you know what?

We don't deserve to make it.

Honestly, the human race deserves to fade.

I realize this ironically sounds like a hallmark card, but it is the truth.

The honest truth is that we're dying.

It's the human condition.

We're all born to self-destruct.

So why do we even exist?

I suppose that question doesn't matter because no one takes the time to even think about it.

And that's the honest truth.

I know that these words are meaningless because they will only fall on blind eyes, but I think I say it all because for the first time I am seeing the world,

The world as it really is.

And I am blown away by the sight.

I am such a lovely girl.

Always the nice and polite one.

Always the peace maker.

Always the guilty one.

Always the sorry one.

I always want to make everyone happy around me, so it would seem.

Infact, everyone likes me because I am the happy one.

Sometimes I feel like I am a joke to everyone.

Sometimes I get so angry that I want to take this image of me and tear it to shreds.

Because no one cares about the shy ones,

The quiet ones,

The pretending ones.

You have never thought twice about me.

Never examined the underneathings of me because you never cared.

I was just that person you could pass by without a second glance.

I was the invisible one.

I am sick of it all because things change and so have I.

But you never see that because you don't care.

You don't see the dull pain.

You don't see the passion inside,

Nor do you see my hopes and dreams.

You see nothing at all in me,

And because of this I believe that I am also nothing.

It doesn't matter if I'm coming or going, you honestly don't care.

I wonder what it would be like sometimes to be taken seriously?

I wonder what it would be like to have people wonder about me?

Most people don't know who I am.

Most wouldn't believe who I am.

How would they react if I finally told them the truth?

When I tore off this mask and ripped down these walls so they could truly see.

It comes out for them and all that was gold is now stained.

Would they stop to stare?

Cringe at the ugly sight?

How am I doing for you now?

Do I have your attention now?

I need to tell you the truth.

I need to show you the lost chapters.

I need to tell you the story of me because I need you to see me just as I really am.

You never knew how deep I went,

And you still don't.

There is no way for you even to measure.

How do you like this now?

Because God knows I have spent my life living for you,

Never myself.

And you didn't give a shit about me anyways.

But it's all going to change now.

You never knew before.

I was too afraid to speak then.

But you will know now.

Come on, let me show you what I'm made of.

To the love...

I want to know if you really love me or not. Not that you are suppose to love me, or because you feel you need to, but do you really? I know that I can be hard to love sometimes. I can be bitchy, moody, self-centered, out-of-control, rude, frustrating, nervous, shy, loud, cold, and hurtful. I can tear you apart in a moment's time. So will you take that chance to love me even though you know it may blow up in your face?

Would you still love me anyway?

I am a wreck sometimes, I know.

I am broken at times.

I am most definitely lost sometimes.

But I am certain of one thing.

In the end, boy,

I have always loved you,

Honestly and truly.

I stand on a mountain.

You are across from me on another mountain.

I think I love you.

We stare at each other but we do not say a word.

We do not speak.

But I look and I see that love may be in your eyes too.

Do you love me?

I guess we will never know.

I am on one mountain.

You are on the other.

And we never come to meet each other in the valley in between.

I hear it's lovely there.

I wish so much you would come to me and tell me what you really think.

Then I could tell you what I think.

We could stop trying to fake it.

We could tell the truth.

But we won't.

You know it and I know it.

We just stare at each other from our peaks.

Our lonely mountains.

Sometimes the air gets so thin on my mountain it's hard to breathe.

I look at you on your mountain and I wonder if you feel that way too.

I think I do honestly love you.

But you will never know.

Still, you are on my mind forever.

Two souls so close and yet so far apart.

Almost there but not quite.

Mr. Waltz waltzes with me to a symphony.

His fingers fit perfectly with mine,

And my heart falls helplessly into the palm of his hand.

He glides me across the black stage and sends me into a twirl.

For the first time in my life I feel beautiful.

He wraps his arm around my waist but I do not let my insecurities get the best of me, instead, I wrap my arm around his shoulder until I am so close to something that is breathing.

Something that is alive.

Someone who could need me.

Someone who could love me.

Mr. Waltz smiles, his dark eyes gleaming, and I fall apart.

But at the end of the dance he tosses me away.

Just a simple laugh escapes from his mouth as though I am nothing to him.

I fall to the stage and my red dress swirls around me.

Mr. Waltz moves to a petite blonde who moves from the behind shadows, the lights focus in on them.

They glow and I descend into darkness.

Tears fall helplessly around me and I hide myself.

Ashamed that I trusted again.

The symphony has died down to just a piano playing softly in the background.

I sit on the stage and watch silently as my song dies softly.

Tears falling, I wish and wait until the next time Mr. Waltz asks for my hand to dance once more.

I realize Mr. Waltz doesn't need me,
But I need Mr. Waltz.
He makes me feel alive,
And I want someone to hold me.

There is love somewhere in a room at this moment.

A love that is being made for the first time.

In this room lies two human beings, two human hearts.

About to give themselves to each other.

Creating a love.

Clothes fall, walls fall, and they create love within that room.

A love that has no greed, no fear, no evil.

Together they lie in a bed made of trust.

This is the first time they fell to this place.

For this, the world quakes.

The same sexes, the different races, the unmarried giving away their virginity.

God, will understand won't he?

Will the world understand?

Because love exists within these moments.

These moments when two souls combine.

I don't care what the religious, the condemning, or you say,

From where I stand,

It's beautiful.

How can you condemn them?

When love is created.

For you,

I think I would die.

I would,

Travel a thousand life times,

Just to find you.

But you,

Are like a precious stone locked away from me.

I see you,

But will never feel you.

But I have dreamed of you and me a thousand times.

I wish on all the stars,

For you,

To love me,

More than anyone you have known before.

I think if I had the chance,

I would,

Write I love you on the sand of a shore,

Just so the waves could take it away,

To the ocean.

My love would then circle the world.

Then would you know,

About me?

The girl who is a shadow.

Who longs secretly to be with you.

I think,

I would die,

For you.

Do you want to know the absolute best and glorious part of a man? There are these two muscles right before the man's butt that I absolutely love. Two hills of muscles that are like two parallel roads. I imagine my hands running down them so gently, ever so softly. But those are two roads I will never know. So it seems that I am alone.

Sitting in the dim light in my room, I am on my bed, just sitting. And a thought suddenly enters into my mind and I ponder on it for just a while. What if you were to come knock on my door, would I let you in? I can imagine your face beyond the glass and I can hear the door creak as I open it slowly. You would come in and I would wrap my arms around you. You would pick me up and take me to my bedroom. Your hand would move slowly across my stomach going downward.

We would not say a word.

And there is love.

Like a stain on white sheets,

There is an essence of love.

Men are not the answer to my troubles,

So why do I even think about them?

Men,

Like as many women as they want to like.

Who would ever bother to look at me?

They always walk past me.

Men,

The only reason they're here is to hurt me, hurt me, and hurt me.

I have wandered around this world looking for the one person I was meant to love. I would not fall for just anyone. I will not fall for any lies because I am looking for something that is real. I am not an easy one unlike every other girl you probably know. They all toss their hair and lick their lips to anyone that passes them by. I, on the other hand, guard my heart with a thousand soldiers. So why did you ever think you could get in so easily? You stood at my gates and waited for me to simply let you in but instead I simply refused you. So you in return found her. The gentle and wonderful soul she is.

Oh and she thinks you are a God.

I, on the other hand, see beyond that.

You lead such a meaningful life now, such a simple life. And she tries desperately to make you happy. She gives you what you want, doesn't she? She's even quiet when you fuck her, isn't she? She fell into the palm of your hand and you can mold her. You get along with her parents, she puts out, she makes you feel like a God, so I imagine you will marry her. And you lead such a simple life. Oh and I bet she has picked out the most magnificent wedding dress.

Such an easy life you will have.

With me, you would have had to hold me down. You would have had to crawl through my webs with me and somehow convince me that you were real. I would have fought it with everything in my body, and you would have had to fight for me. We would have wrestled and fought each other, circling around. You would have had to make me fall. But you took the easy way out,

You found her.

She makes you happy, doesn't she? Holding hands, butterfly kisses, and ice cream. You live in such a simple world now, don't you?

But what about passionate? Do you have a passionate life? Do you really want to wake up in the morning?

Does she fill that lust you have? Does she scratch her nails down your back and bit your neck? Does she cause a tension in you that makes your heat rise? Does she excite you?

I'm sure she must, after all, she thinks so highly of you.

After all, you guys have been together for so long and she fits into your life so perfectly.

She was so easy for you to get.

I was hard so you threw in the towel and took the easy way out.

We played games with each other, circled and infuriated each other.

Backed away and ran away from each other.

But that flame was there.

Do you remember it in my eyes when I looked at you?

I wouldn't be so easy for you, instead, I would defy you.

For my love I wanted to make you fight.

I wanted you to capture me.

I wanted you to fight.

But you didn't and because of this you missed it.

You missed everything I had to give. The mornings, the afternoons, and the nights. The love I have been saving for so long. The passion I had for you. I thought about standing outside of your window and screaming your name until you answered me, but you aren't worth it. You don't care so I don't care. You do nothing so I will do nothing in return. I want to save my strength for someone that's worth fighting for. That tension that existed before has now turned into something different, something ugly. I suppose if I could find any way to have revenge on you I would take it.

Just to piss you off.

We could never be you know. You're too damn dull and I want someone who excites me. Someone who will run through this life with me. Someone who is willing to fight for me. I want someone who is strong and will stand up to me because I am not being taken so easily. And you only can stand things if they're easy.

But I hope you have a nice, dull, simple life with your future wife.

Sometimes I get scared that there is nobody in this world who is meant to love me. Do you ever feel that way too? I'm so scared no one will want me. I have spent all my life feeling as if I wasn't wanted. Will no one ever look and see the woman within me? Sometimes I feel so ugly inside and out. How could I make them stay around? When of all the things I could wish for I would wish for a chance to be anyone but me. I just want someone to complete my soul.

I want my soul mate.

I want to look into his eyes and know that for the rest of my life I will not be alone. I want to look at him and feel him around me. His breath on my body. His love wrapping circles around me. I want to know that it will last till the end of time.

But who's going to want me?

When I am such a wreck. When there are so many other girls out there who are so much greater than I. I am just one woman. One simple woman who wants to love someone. I stand here alone,

Waiting for the words.

"Colleen, there are millions of girls, but I like you most of all. I choose you out of all the people."

Wouldn't that be nice?

I think if that ever happened to me I wouldn't be able to breathe.

Can two hearts meet again after they leave each other?

They brushed each other for a moment and then walked by.

Can that feeling last until they meet again?

Will the world keep moving or will it stop and start only when these two people meet for a second time?

Can there be a thing called destiny?

Can there truly only be one person who is made for me?

Can you honestly look at someone and say, "I have loved you from the very first moment I saw you."

Can something that great exist?

I wonder if you ever wondered about it too?

I wonder if you ever thought of me that way?

I think maybe, just maybe, time will bring you back to me.

What do you think of it all?

Because when I brushed your hand today with mine,

Something in the wind changed.

When I'm worlds away from you.

Will you know it?

Will you feel it?

Will you feel like someone is watching you?

Like someone is following you wherever you go.

Like there is someone always two steps behind.

Will you feel a prick on your neck, like a breath of a person?

Will you hear my whisper into your ear?

Will you see me down the street?

Will I be gone when you take a second look?

Will you always know that no matter where I go in this world you will always cross my mind?

Always.

Even if I'm worlds away.

Here is the past love life of Colleen Cherwinski:

Love Interest One: This boy was the first boy I ever thought I truly was in love with. It was in the first grade and he was in the same class as me. He used to be obsessed with turtlenecks and I suppose I was obsessed with black stretch pants. We were the perfect couple. I used to sit by him, and tell him how much I was in love with him. The whole class knew it, I knew it, and he knew it. I suppose this is the only time in my life when I have had a relationship that actually worked out. Unfortunately it happened in the first grade and by the time second grade arrived he was much too popular for me. I became invisible. But I was not shaken or stirred, instead, I gently moved on. Maybe it was because I was young or maybe it was because I hadn't developed my insecurities.

Love Interest Two: He came to our school around third grade and the first time I saw him I knew that I was in love with him. He was the athletic, good looking kid. I was the now shy, slightly chubby girl that secretly loved him from afar. It really wasn't a secret though. He knew it and so did his friends, and I became the biggest joke to them. Every time I would walk by, even if it were for no particular reason at all, his friends would yell, "Look, here she comes!" Was I truly that disgusting? I still look back on those days and I wish I could have a little revenge. But back then I liked him even if he was a bastard.

Love Interest Three: I started to notice him when a teacher made a comment that she thought he would grow up to be the best looking guy in high school. Suddenly, I saw exactly what she was talking about. I got to him through a friend. Immediately, I knew he didn't like me, but I think he felt like he had to pretend because I was trying so hard. I knew it too. At our seventh grade Halloween dance he asked me to dance. I will never forget it because I can still remember the way his breath felt on my neck as I laid my head on his shoulder. I can still feel his stomach as it touched mine as we circled that dance floor. Nobody, as dumb as it may seem, has ever danced with me like that before. I suppose then nobody could hold a candle to him. He ended up asking me out after that dance, I said yes. An hour later he dumped me and I was crushed. The next day he asked me out again and then a week later we were split forever. But in the end, I know it was because he just didn't like me the way I liked him. I always wondered why. Why the hell didn't he like me? I could never figure it all out even today.

At those seventh and eighth grade dances no one hardly asked me to dance. I was a wallflower unlike what I had dreamed I would be when I was younger.

Love Interest Four: I told someone I liked him. They told him about me. He gave me a look over and told all of his friends he thought I was a dog. I cried for an entire week. But then again, I thought maybe he was right, maybe I was a dog.

Love Interest Five: Now this boy was a real Catholic boy. I liked him just because he seemed to listen to me when I talked. He fell in love with everyone but me. I still don't know why I never appealed to him. I suppose this might have been the time in my life when I was sick of getting rejected.

Love Interest Six: He made it clear that he was into me but then I realized that he was into anything that had a vagina. I liked him no matter how much he would flirt with me and then move to the next girl. But he didn't feel the same. Why not? What a fucking player. This is about the time in my life when I got sick of getting hurt.

Love Interest Seven: I think I wanted this one because he was a bastard in the first place. He hated everyone and everything, but was he ever good on stage. At drama he would stand on the stage and I swear everything and everyone would stop to stare at him. I mostly wanted to tear his clothes off. I wanted him to love me. But I suppose he could never love me as much as his on and off girlfriend. I began to wonder if it's my body that doesn't get me anywhere. Am I fat? I hear the Zone diet is good. Maybe the secrets of the world will be revealed to me if I lost ten pounds.

Love Interest Eight: Is the one guy that I have a hard time talking about. He was the first guy that liked me for me. He was emotionally there for me and made it clear that he would take care of me. When I look back on him, I realized that he was the one I think I wanted the most. Ironically, he is the one I ran from. I ran away until the day we both graduated. He was the first person I ever showed myself to and I ran away. Sometimes I can't figure out if I love him or I hate him. What's wrong with me?

So I sit here in the present day telling you about my past loves, my past hurts. It's funny to look back at the way I once was: opened minded and loving, and now look at the way I am now: closed off and scared. I suppose the reason anything goes to complete hell in life is because you get scared. You lose your trust and you develop your unbreakable insecurities and that is exactly what I have done to myself. I am hiding, I admit it. There is always that overwhelming feeling that if I trust someone they will hurt me.

I have always associated the idea of love with hurt. Sometimes I wonder what it would be like if love actually felt good. I think I am done running away. I need to take a break from all this, but if I decide to try the idea of love again someday,

Please don't hurt me.

Even though I know getting hurt is the only way to get through life, I'm just so tired. I don't want to feel that way ever again.

There are some nights,

Some silence nights when I can feel arms around me,

And a breath on my neck that makes me warm.

And I don't feel alone.

And I wonder with all the depths of my soul what it would be like to have someone to hold me.

Someone to touch me.

Would you hold me if I asked you politely?

Just for a moment so I could know what it's like,

To be loved.

To be wanted.

I just want to feel you on my skin.

There is a moment.

There is a moment when one looks at another person and love is built.
There is one moment when someone suddenly looks good. When someone
says the right words to make you notice. When the light reflects off their
body into your eyes. Their presence is felt and you notice when they are
near you.

There is one moment when two worlds collide and love is created.

Just one simple moment,

And the world is never the same.

And I find that I am sadden and lonely because there has not been a person
to have a moment on me.

Why have I not been so lucky?

No moments of love ever come to me, and that is a mystery I wonder about
everyday. For sometimes, I wonder when a moment does come my way, if it
ever does, will I now it?

Though you couldn't probably tell by the way I write about it, I am sick to death of love.

Is there even love out there?

Bleeding heart, crying eyes, do I even care that I will ever love?

I watch people fall in love around me, but not me.

Am I not meant for something so great?

I hate the pain of not having someone who wants to be around me.

I hate the lonliness at night when I lay alone in my bed. I feel the space next to me,

It's empty.

If I never truly fall in love this lifetime,

Will I always be empty?

I want desperately to be wanted.

I want to be loved.

So I keep on trying, but if you brake something so many times,

Eventually it will shut down completely.

You hurt me,

You bastard,

Stop hurting me.

You swore you didn't ever want to see me get hurt, and yet, it was you who did the hurting in the end. I tried being honest with you and it got me nowhere. I took a chance and just like everybody else it blow up in my face. I run away and hide because I wanted you to be different from all the others,

But you weren't.

I am boiling with frustration and anger because you hurt me and I fucking hate being hurt. I thought if I took the chance this time I would get somewhere but for reasons like: I'm ugly, you're spineless, the world doesn't want us to be or I'm not good enough, I didn't get you.

And I wanted you so very badly.

Just leave her, I want to be everything that you wish she was.

Why am I nothing in your world?

Why am I always so easy to brush away?

It's just like everyone else.

No one wants me.

I'm not good enough.

You're killing me and you don't care.

I stood outside and waited for you. I whispered your name and closed my eyes.

Nothing.

Was I not deserving?

Am I just not worthy of love or anything in this world that could actually make me feel good about myself?

And I am hurt.

I listen to Patsy Cline's song "Crazy" over and over, and I drown myself in Swiss cake rolls.

You made me cry on my bed,

Late at night,

Thinking of all the things I did wrong.

What were the words I should have said to make you change your mind about me? I am tired of writing about how absolutely wonderful you are when you turned out to be like everyone else.

And you hurt me,

And then when you were done tearing me apart you calmly walked away.

I'm angry because I ache.

I'm angry because I am a fool.

And I guess I wanted to tell you the one thing I think everyone wishes they could say to the one person who just walked away.

You missed it.

I was willing to love you more than you have ever known before and you let it slip away. I hope you read this and just want to die. I hope you have regret and longing. I hope I haunt your every dream,

And yet, I don't mean that at all.

I just want to let you go, that's all.

I don't want to ache this way anymore.

I want to experience love without getting hurt.

I just want to get over you, because God knows,

I'm not over you.

There is no off and on switch for the way I still feel about you,

And it's killing me.

Ah shit, I'm crying again.

Hey baby, I hear there are reasons why things happen in your life. I hear that people enter your life for reasons that no one knows. You entered and now you walk away, what was your reasoning?

For all that I don't know, I wish to know it all about you. Why do you come, why do you go, and why do I seem to care at all? Who knows the reasons? So I guess I may never know the reasons you entered into me and now you feel you have to walk away.

But hey baby, I wrap it all into a kiss, which I aim to the skies for you.

Here's to all the sunsets we'll miss.

You will always be my,

Would have,

Could have,

Might have.

I wish so much that I could have been with you.

And I think,

You're wonderful.

And I imaged us rolling on the floor together.

It's just too bad.

We would've had so much to laugh about.

My would have,

Could have,

Might have,

We should have been.

It has been so long since the last time I spoke to you that I have forgotten what your voice sounds like. But I know that if I were to hear your voice again, I would know it was you. To tell you a story, just the other day I was sitting on my bed as I am now, writing as I am now, thinking about you as I am now, when something hit my window. One, two, three taps, and I thought it must be you.

You finally came to me.

You finally came running down my street, you finally came to rescue me, finally came to your senses, finally fell in love with me. And I imagined your car waiting outside still running. I would run outside and get in. You would drive us to the Detroit airport and we would fly away together.

To a new life.

And you loved me, even though I may be a tad bit screwed up.

But when I finally pulled back the curtains, you were not there.

It was only the wind.

The snow fell outside the dark glass. It's been so long since I talked to you. I think the last time I saw you and the last time I said anything to you I said, " See ya." If I had known how I still think about you and if I had known that was it, that was the last and final time you would hear me speak, I wouldn't have said a word. I would have took you by the hand, took you up to your bedroom, lifted my blue dress, unzipped your pants and let you make a moment.

Because I miss you.

I would have not just walked away. I would have stayed and together we would have made a reason for you to talk to me again.

" See ya."

What did it sound like to you? Is it an echo in your mind today? Did you know that it was the last chance?

I did not.

There is this great sadness that exists within me, because of all the things I could have done, I did nothing. So there is just so much wondering that I spend my time, writing, life thinking about it.

I honestly always thought if there ever was a time in the world when I needed someone, or if I needed someone to talk things over with, I could always run to you. But now, you only run from me. So who will I need? Who will I run to when I have no one?

Not you anymore.

And here, I always thought I'd be safe with you.

I realize that when I stated my affections to you there would be consequences but I never thought I would lose everything. I spoke the honest truth and now I am being punished for it. You were supposed to always be there for me. I always thought you would. I never thought you had the nerve to simply write me out of your life.

I was simply wrong.

I had built you so much in my dreams and I am sad that you have decided I am too much of a burden. Nothing I said, wrote, or thought matters anymore. It just comes down to the simple fact that you were a trusted friend, a person I revealed myself to and cared about, and you aren't anymore.

You won't be there when I need someone. You don't care. You will never be able to stand in a room with me without the noticed wall you have created. You aren't going to rescue me. You aren't going to be the one to not give up on me.

All you give is lonely nights.

You are no lover, not even a friend, only an awkward stranger to me now who refuses to be there when I am falling apart.

And you're gone.

It's over, it's really truly over. Oh, how long have I been in denial.

I guess I always thought I'd talk to you once more.

Oh wait, was that love passing me by?

No, it seems it was just the wind.

So I guess I'll see ya.

I stood on the end of my driveway.

I waited for you.

I wore my white dress and my dancing shoes.

I wanted to dance with you in the pouring rain.

Let the liquid silver wash away all our worries.

I wanted to walk with you on the highest mountains.

I wanted to run through the fields and lay in the middle of the world with you.

I wanted to laugh and cry with you.

I wanted to feel your breath on my body.

I called your name out to the sky hoping you would hear me.

I waited at the end of my driveway,

I waited at the end of the world for you,

But you never came.

To the happiness,

And the ways things are going to be...

I know that I am young.

Not worth any attention.

I'm not forty going through a mid-life crisis.

I am not dying.

I am not a subject of a bad childhood nor am I a drug addict.

I'm not worth the pain of worrying.

You really don't want to listen to me of all the people you could listen to.

But I am here too.

I know that you think that people like me are too young to know what heart ache is.

I haven't experienced enough.

I haven't been here long enough nor have I hurt enough.

But I know that deep down I am every forty year old who wakes up one day to find their life isn't going the way they wanted it to. I am a woman who is dying. I think I die inside when I live a day that has no meaning. I had moments that were so low I couldn't pick myself off the floor because I was sobbing so hard. I look at my body and I wish I could wash away half of myself in the shower. Sometimes I feel old like I have lived on this earth for so long and it's beat me. Then I feel the dimness of hope of the seventeen year old girl that I am.

I know you don't believe that I could know what it all means,

Because I don't.

I'm lost just like you.

You say I'll get it all when I'm older.

You'll say before I die it'll all make sense to me.

But sometimes when I look in the mirror I see someone who could have the power to find it all.

To have the strength to learn now.

In the end, there is only one life and I'm tired of waiting.

My hope is that someday I might possess the strength of a woman whose been here for many years beyond me.

Where do all the dreamers go?

Can someone please tell me?

That is where I belong,

Because I dream my life away.

Don't you see?

I just don't want to live an ordinary life.

For all the countless reasons,

I just want something to live for.

An odd day, an odd day indeed to have a revelation.

I had to do it because it was my job. I was an aide for the library and I needed to take some books to a classroom. When I arrived no one was in the room. I put the books on the teacher's desk without noticing anything, but when I turned around I stopped. I was surprised to find that I was staring at a life I used to know. A life I had forgotten. That room I walked into was an old classroom of mine when I was young. My eyes immediately moved to the desk where I used to sit and I felt as though I was still in that room, like I had left something behind. I could feel my old self around me. The air was just the way it had been before. The feelings and the atmosphere were also the same. I stood there for a moment and breathed in the air I did as a child.

And then she was there.

Skinny, long brown hair, blue eyes. Could you believe it was me? Years younger and staring me with a hunger. She smiled but I was terrified. I could see her reaching her hand out for me to take it, so I did. She stared at me with a longing I had grown to know all to well. Funny how some things never change.

When I look at pictures of the girl I used to be I wish I could be her again. I could be young and untouchable the way I used to be. I was so unbelievably joyful and so trusting. I wasn't depressed or lonely, I was just living. When you get older everyone says, "You have to grow up." Suddenly, you can't do half of the things you used to do and you forgot what it felt like to be the way you used to be, you forget the joy. As I stared at myself I realized that I was staring at everything I wanted to be again.

The weatherman said tomorrow is suppose to be the hottest day this spring. I think tomorrow I'll put on my bathing suit and run through the sprinkler.

Just like I would have done years ago. I miss it and I realize when I let go
of that little girl's hand that day and left her in that room I did leave
something behind,

Myself.

There was this girl once upon a time who dreamed a world for herself. Everyone around her said she was out of her mind. She was impractical and foolish. She was not like everyone else. This girl felt more than anyone ever to breathe. Her soul racked earthquakes through her body and told her that they were wrong. This girl listened to her heart beat out a pattern. A pattern that was never heard before. A life that was a dream. But one day this girl woke to find her dream was her life.

Every time you close your eyes can you see what could happen?

The wind blew my simple face.

This simple life has been circling me.

I breathed it in today.

I love life,

Even when it gets hard.

Even when I'm bad at it.

It makes me feel alive.

Mostly because I love the scent.

The scent of life.

The scent of my life,

A shattered fragment of a gray sky.

If you ever wanted to know a useless piece of information about my childhood, here it is: I had a hard time spending the night at other girls' houses when I was littler. I would brake out into tears and my parents would have to come and take me home. I remember at one of my friend's houses I was having another episode. It was late and her grandma woke up to find me crying. I sat there on a bed and hide my face underneath the covers. She sat next to me and pulled the covers down so she could see me face.

"Colleen, don't be ashamed. It's just that you feel a little more than other's do."

That was the very first night I got through. I never forgot that woman. The absolute kindness she showed, or the words she said. It felt almost to me like she had touched on something that no one had ever touched on before. It's just a useless small thing in life, but I find it crossing my mind every now and then.

If I could have one thing right now,

It would most definitely be,

The most amazing pair of red high heels.

Four-inch heels in fire engine red.

All the women who never get hurt wear them.

That is the reason to wish for,

A spectacular pair of red high heels.

What remains of the day is always nothing. There is a time when I think about the day and I realized that it was useless. A rain drop in a bucket, it was just another day to me.

I fought, I cried, I lost, I had realizations, I lived and loved. I had been alive for another day, but when the dusk came and settled all around me, I stopped to examine the contents of what I had done throughout the day and it seems that I had missed my expectations.

If life is suppose to be a wonder and if life is suppose to be an always happy experience, then I am missing the point at which it all must begin.

For what remains of the day is a longing. Always the longing of that idea that maybe tomorrow will be that day when it all falls to place.

And when the night comes and I see the stars are still placed in the sky, just as they should be, I wonder,

What remains of my life?

When I only have a certain amount of time to do all I know I must do. When the day always goes by so fast and I am rushed and tired. The night is so long, holding my mind on one question,

What remains of this life of mine?

My eyes fall upon the stars that are there each night, just as they should be. And through their wonder I create my very own wonder. This moment, this very second, maybe I was not where I wanted to be, but maybe I was where I should be.

Always the longing.

I long for the answers to this world.

I wish to know I have not been mistaken.

Joan of Arc was born to parents of the French peasant class. In May 1428, the voices of St. Michael and St. Catherine Margaret told Joan to go to the King of France and help him reconquer the kingdom. This seventeen year old girl (my age exactly) was given a small army. She then enjoyed series of spectular military successes during which the king was able to be crowned with her by his side. In May 1430, she was captured by the Burgundians and sold to the English. When Joan refused to retract the assertion that it was the saints of God that commanded her to do what she had done, she was condemned to death. She was burned at the stake on May 30th, 1431.

She was only nineteen when she died.

Sometimes I feel selfish. I look about this world and I see the dying and suffering. People are falling and people are losing. There are so many people out in this world doing things that are so great, and I sit here and complain about my meaningless life.

In the end, I am just one girl caught in with others exactly like me.

We all long to be great.

We all have the strength to do great things in our lives, so I hear.

If Joan of Arc can lead a revolution at the age of seventeen,

I can get out of bed in the morning.

I trail my fingers down my inner thighs ever so slowly. Listening to Jimi Hendrix softly on the radio in my room.

Lately, I feel like Madonna.

I put my mirror on my bed so I can look at myself. I want to see what I will look like from the other end. And I move my hips to the music.

I imagine a man in the corner of my room. He is dark with no face, but his clothes are still on. I suppose for me to rip them off.

I lick my lips and move my hand across my chest. I imagine pushing him against the wall and making him touch the parts I have longed for someone to touch for so long.

I watch my body in the mirror and I look different. The light reflects off it.

I bite my fist like it is a man's shoulder. I feel hands on my body.

Heat running through me.

I can feel the dimness and the soft lips trail across my body. Passion and pulses of heat.

The guitar hits a shrilled high note, and it sends an electric wave through my body. Swirling me and taking me.

I feel steam rise inside my body as it rocks to the drums in the back line of the music. When that last eerie note plays, I find that I am sweaty. I look in the mirror that shows me a woman that nobody knows.

A passionate woman.

A sexual woman.

She looks at me and laughs. "If they only knew, Colleen." She laughs and bites her finger.

I take a shower and wash away all feelings of wrong. The water is hot, and I foolishly trail my fingers down every point on my body. I bite my lip lightly.

I feel it again.

God help me, I can't help it anymore.

Oh shit, I forgot we weren't suppose to talk about sex. All the conservatives calling their local priests now. I think somewhere deep inside I have always wanted to take people like that, chew them up, and then spit them out. But then again, I'm suppose to wait until I'm married or I'll burn in the fires of hell. I must not say a word about how good this one spot on my body feels to touch. I must not fantasize about men in my bedroom. I must keep all feelings to myself. I am not, under any circumstances, suppose to talk about sex. I've got to lock all thoughts in my head.

If I talk about sex then I am a slut, and I will give my family a bad name. We all call the girl around us that sleeps with all the men a whore, but secretly we wish to be her. To feel the way she feels everyday. I am wrong, so the world tells me. But I am secretly busting out of my seams. Laughing at my virginity. Thinking if only the guys in high school had known what I was thinking as they walked by, I would have kissed my virginity goodbye.

I get pointers from movies and magazines about how to make a man feel like a king. The right way to go down on a guy is a trait that every woman should know. Where can I buy a dildo? Are there any cheap prositutes around? No one says. No one speaks about sex really. Maybe in a whisper when you are talking with your girlfriends, or on a television show at 2:00 AM in the morning. There are condoms in the right aisle, try not to feel to ashamed when you buy them. Parents talk to their children, well, kind of. They teach us well in health class, well, sort of. Television and movie stars tell us more. Kids want to do it in order to feel older, teenagers what to do it because they want someone, and adults do it because they feel like it is what they are suppose to do. But the main reason sex flourishes through the world, I think in the end, is because we all just want someone to be close to and we want to feel good.

Everyone is lost, so I have found out. No one talks about anything, so casual sex runs wild. Aids kill people, and yet, no one talks still. A girl gets pregnant because she was too ashamed to go on the pill. Masturbation is a dirty word that only is meant to be made fun of, but no one says that in the end, it might be the best solution.

It's funny, everyone swears that everyone is open in this world. But God forbid I make love to a black man, that would ruin the perfect image of sex. That would be a scandal, because I might fall in love with that black man. Everyone smiles to my face, but if I should ever find that I liked girls more than men, they wouldn't be smiling any more. It's a common rule in this world: Same race, different sexes. They all imagine the action and they shiver with the thought because supposedly it's wrong to do it any other way. I'm wrong. The world's wrong. So everyone sits around and never says a word about it all even though we crave sex because we all want to feel good again and sex is the easiest and cheapest way to get that temporary high.

Shit.

Sorry, I forgot that we weren't suppose to talk about how the people in this world refuse to change even though the world is changing around them. Or how much cheap, unprotected, unspoken, unshameful but yet unreasonable, unholy, let's-do-it-to-be-cool, unforgivable and yet ironically beautiful banging goes on around here.

She wakes early in the morning and puts on her shorts and an old shirt. I am still nestled in my bed. Sometimes when she knows it is going to be hot she'll wear the hat that I bought for her.

My mother really loves flowers.

All types. She even took a class on them just so she could learn their names and where best they would all grow. She has always wanted to open up a nursery.

My mother cares about the things she plants.

She spends her free time from work watering her plants. She pulls weeds for hours and asks for my opinion on if her wreath is straight on the house. Then she fills it in with flowers.

Every spring she plants these bushes by our house, and God, when they bloom they are the most beautiful thing I have ever seen, and suddenly our house is like a dream. Everything looks beautiful. When my mother is away I usually have to water her plants. I stare at each pot and each bush, but I know roses are her favorite. Out of all the flowers in the world, my mother has found the time to find the one she likes the best. Who in their life can say they have truly done that?

My mother also likes tomatoes.

She has a garden that produces, I swear, a hundred tomatoes a year. She likes them with salt. I wish you could see her eyes when she brings in all the things she has grown from her garden. They look alive.

She is passionate about her flowers and her garden. She wakes up and she has a reason to. Something needs her outside of her window. So she can spend hours working and tending, while I on the other hand, usually wake up from a long sleep and feel dead. I look at her through our back window. I think that if she had the chance she would spend the rest of her life with her flowers and her garden. I swear I don't have the patience for that sort of

122

thing, but secretly? I wish, I wish so much that I was like my mother. I wish I cared about something so passionately that it was all I ever wanted to do with my life. Because then that would give me a reason to wake up and feel alive. To wake up and feel the sun on my back, and the feeling of satisfaction. To have a reason just to be here.

God, that would be so great.

My dad is a funny man.

He likes to tell me that I have it well off.

He likes to tell me about how hard things were for him when he was my age.

He likes to remind me that I have it easy.

He likes to tell me about how they had to walk sixty miles to school without any shoes on. Or how he had to slide down a massive hill in the snow without any pants on just to catch the bus. One time he got lost so he had to eat his own foot for food.

Just kidding.

He doesn't say it really quite that way,

But sometimes it feels like that to me.

But really dad,

I know already.

I do have it good.

So do you.

Everything's good.

If I had a million dollars I would give you whatever you wanted.

        Buy myself a car and drive until it was all left behind.

Build my mom a garden full of roses, buy my dad a football team, build my brother a golf course,

        Piss away my dreams.

If I had a million dollars, I'd buy some nicer clothes and I would get lipo on my ass and thighs.

These are just a few of the things I would do if I had a million dollars.

So it turns out that the world doesn't like girls with A sized breasts. So my friend, who also has A sized boobs like me, and I went to Wal-Mart because we wanted to buy enhancing bras so we could be loved by the world. I picked a red frilly one, which only ended up to be three dollars. I bought a thong too.

"Do these things weigh a lot?" The cashier asked me, talking about my new jelly bra.

"No, not really. They do give me boobs though." I said back.

"I know, I never had boobs until I got pregnant," She said, "but don't go out and get pregnant just to get boobs, that's stupid."

I suppose that is the real reason I wrote this all down.

As far back as I can possibly remember I have wanted to be everything to you. I want to make you happy and proud of me. I want to fulfill the dreams and expectations that you have planned for me. I want to be perfect for you. I want to be the essence of all that I should be in your eyes. Can I measure up to the high standards?

I want to be good for you.

So I try so hard for you. Can you see the strain in me? I try to make you proud. I hurry up for you, because I want you to look at me in that light when you are happy with something I do. But I have a confession.

I have been screwing up lately, horribly so.

I have been losing focus on my goals. I stop in the road and search for a way out.

You say there is no pressure. Everything is up to me, and yet I find myself always wanting to please you. Every decision that I make, I make for you. So is this endless feeling of despair because I need to make one for me. You say you like me just the way I am.

As long as I make up for what you blew, right?

I have to ask you, would everything be fine if for just once I did what I pleased even if it all falls apart in the end?

Just once.

Would that be okay with you?

And in the end will you still love me?

Would you still love me even if…

I never made anything great of myself.

I fell apart and never regained myself.

I gained thirty pounds and kept it.

I screwed up everything.

I never stop acting nervous.

I never stopped crying.

I clung to you and never let go.

I dreamed my life away.

Everything I did wasn't good enough.

I woke up to realize that I was wrong about everything.

I went bankrupt.

I lost my hair and my humor.

I never knew the right thing to say.

I never acted normal around people.

I went completely insane.

I hid in the corner the rest of my life.

I really wonder if you could.

Looking at my senior picture of a girl who smiles, she looks so happy.

She smiles but is she really happy?

If you look into the eyes of a person you will see a soul. Is that soul just pretending? Do you think that soul feels happiness?

I feel like I have been too harsh on some people in my life. I feel as though I have passed judgment too quickly and not looked beyond the surface.

Look beyond the surface.

How I wish someone would consider this on me. Sometimes I want to do the same but do not. There is always more to this, more to me, more to the people I have judged throughout my life.

No, this is not a safe way to live life, assuming everything is good, but no way is safe.

Simply look beyond the surface.

What I am trying to say is,

Forget assumptions,

Open your eyes,

Not everything is what it seems.

Women are not supposed to have deep thoughts. Women are suppose to be perfect. We, after all, have been trying to perfect ourselves for years. We are supposed to cook meals that actually taste good. Women are sensitive and always caring. They are most definitely in love with love. Women are considered bitches if they are driven. Boy, I'll make you wish you were dead if you get in my way. I suppose I'm proud to be developing my bitchy side. All the push over women get trampled by all the other women. If a woman laughs too much she is considered dumb. But who honestly cares if we're dumb or not, woman are great lovers too. Passionate and loving, we will take care of you. I think I am a true woman because I find myself wanting someone to take care of. I think I must be a true woman because I have already picked out my wedding dress, and yet, wouldn't it be nice if I could just be single my whole life? But that's just not what women do. Sometimes I think I need to take a break from all the expectations and all the obligation so I can breathe. Take off my bra, don't shave my legs, forget about wearing any make-up, and find out who I am and what I'm really trying to do here.

If there is something about women to know it would be we are all were born to be feminists. Now it's true, some are angrier than others, but we still have the same qualities inside of us.

I admit it, I'm a feminist. I am a woman and sometimes I feel little compared to men. Sometimes I feel like the main goal in a woman's life is to find a man.

It's a man's world.

So I feel this great need to take control and prove it all wrong. Granted, most people think feminists hate men, but I would have to say that I love men.

The world wouldn't be the same without them.

But I do admit that when I see a woman kicking a man's ass I laugh, but only quietly.

I smile, but just a little.

Mona,

Mona,

You snobby double-faced bitch.

You are the essence of all that a woman should not be.

You describe yourself out to be a Greek goddess.

You fly through life on the backs of everyone else.

Someday I swear it, Mona, I'll step on you like a bug.

Mona, I'll owe your ass,

And everything else you have.

You over dramatic, whiny, fake, half stupid, ignorant, slut-like, piece of woman.

I pray that I will someday be free of you, Mona.

You have no grace and no dignity.

Your comments make me livid with anger.

You think you got it all figured out.

You think everyone's under your little thumb, especially all the men.

But Mona, when it all comes down upon you,

I'll be there to laugh at you.

I guess you should try harder, Mona, not to talk so much about yourself next time.

You'll never get a man or friends that way.

You really are a bitch,

Mona.

I walked into my senior prom and found unlike what I had thought I wasn't the most beautiful girl in the world. I felt completely out of place, a feeling I have grown accustomed to. Something inside of me was saying, "You don't belong here anymore." I have always wondered why the guys never asked me to slow dance with them. I guess I will only be left to wonder. No one asked me to dance. I am a wallflower.

I've always been a wallflower, it's another thing I'm accustomed to. I wish sometimes I could have one of those moments when I did something completely out of control. I wish I had gotten on a table and danced.

But I didn't.

There is so much left that I just didn't do.

After an hour of sitting around, attempting to dance, and standing by the punch bowl so it would look like I fit in I think I figured something out.

I don't fit in.

So I left that dance. I ran past the DJ, the boy I loved, the lights, the tinsel, and to the world outside. A gentle wind swirled around me and I breathed it in like it was the first breath I ever took. I stood outside and looked at the midnight sky.

I don't want to be here anymore.

I don't want to feel this way anymore.

So I made a wish that night.

I went to a small catholic school in a small unknown town in northern Michigan. In this school, we were taught about Jesus, about how to be the elite of the world, and how to survive. We had it well off to the rest of the world. The good catholic children we were. Beneath the squeaky clean surface lived a new generation. Alcoholics, whores, and outsiders, that is what we were deep down.

I went to a catholic school that taught us about God and ways to get in to heaven.

I learned about the world there, and we were tested to be the best.

To be individuals but still follow their rules.

Somewhere the students decided they did not want to be individuals and that they wanted to be like everyone else.

You now belonged to a certain group. There were ranks among the people and you usually knew where you stood in the line of things. I kept to myself even though I was screaming inside.

Through the masses I found that I did not fit and I did not like being in a place where I just did not belong.

So for years I was hidden, the truth of me was a secret, because I was oddly different and oddly out of place. So I was a secret that went unnoticed.

It was an awkward time of happiness, of pain, of dreaming. Finally when it came to an end, they stamped their seal of approval on your forehead and threw you out into the light of the world.

We all stood in line looking at through the door of the world, blinded by its light, looking exactly like one another. Through the maddening crowd, I saw the world for the first time and I saw the difference in me compared to the others.

I saw that I was different.

I was different and that was okay.

134

The canvas was clean and I have since forgotten the reasons I ever doubted myself back then. No, they didn't see it then.

They didn't see the secret of me,

Will they see it now?

Do you ever wish that you could run as fast as you could through a field in the middle of nowhere just so you could lay there on the grass and stare up at the sky above you? To look at your life as you twist your fingers around the grass beside you?

To feel alive?

I am beginning to realize that the world is made up of two kinds of people. Those people who are lost and those who are found. The ones who are lost are the ones out for the money. The ones who wake up every morning and feel dead. They sigh too loud and cry harder than anyone else. You can see the sorrow in their eyes. You can see the dull pain. They aren't living life anymore, they are just being alive. They forget to breathe. They forget to laugh and forgive. When they check their mail they find mostly bills, but secretly, they wish the mail would bring them news of a better life. The best advice they can give you is to marry rich. They are the lost looking to be found.

The ones who are found are the people everyone wishes themselves to be. They always have a laugh and a smile on their lips. They have found themselves and they have learned to accept life and they love it just the way it is. They have the right clothes, the right house, and the right attitude. They know the things in the world that make them the most happy. They stay away from things that make them lose their way. They live the life they dreamed of. They do the little things. They are the people who run through fields as fast as they can just so they can look up at the sky.

Lately, I think I'm lost. I think I'm letting the world take me and mold me into whatever it wants me to be. I realize that it is my duty to go to college, find a job and make money, find a spouse and grow old. But is that all?

I think there is something missing in my life, but I don't know what it is. I don't know where to even start the search. But I've been thinking a lot lately that most of all I want to be one of the few who are found.

To the reader:

Do you care about any of this at all? It's just that sometimes I find myself wondering if any of the stuff I write about matters at all to you. I really don't know why it would. You probably get sick of me cursing the world all the time, don't you? So do I. I just wanted to tell you how I have been feeling lately. I haven't told a lot of people that. I guess I wanted to tell you the truth because I don't think anyone knows the truth about my life. I honestly don't think I knew the truth either until I started to write this for you. But do you care?

Can I tell you the simple things that I worry about the most? Sometimes I feel like my life isn't complicated or dramatic enough for anyone to care about. I am just a simple average woman who just woke up one day and found that she was empty. I wonder sometimes if my writings aren't fancy enough. I look at writings that are so great, and then I look at mine. Am I just a joke? Do you think this is stupid and not worth your time? I never thought I was the type of person who needed validation from anyone, and yet, I need it from you. I need your understanding and I need your compassion. I want you to walk up to me on the street and tell me that you know exactly how I feel. That all of this makes sense. I am not alone. My words, though they may be simple and short, mean something to you, don't they? Does any of this mean anything? It's just that I'm trying so hard to get it right for you and sometimes I doubt myself. I doubt my abilities, and I doubt that you care at all about anything I have to say. Well if it all goes to hell, thank you for at least reading this far into this. I don't think you realize that it means the world to me. I wanted to ask you a question and I wanted you to take the time to think about it. If I continued to write this for the rest of my life would you mind? It's just that this is the first time I have honestly felt good about myself.

All that I ever wanted rests in a quaint bookstore downtown. It is one of those stores that you step in and it just feels right. You feel as if you are meant to be there.

If you come in through the front door and turn to your right, you will find a white circle shaped display stand with all the latest book on it. I feel desperate every time I look at this particular stand of books,

Because that is all I ever wanted.

All I want is to have my own book on that table. I want to come in on a Sunday afternoon and step through the front door and head to that display stand. There will be my new book, two or three copies of it. I want to smile because a dream has come true, and yet, the world will be silent around me as though it is just watching me. I want to pick up my book and smell it's pages, read my name in gold on the front cover and know that it belongs to me. Then I want to set it back down on that round table to be sold to someone who will care about it.

All I want is people to read about my life and care.

That is all I truly desire in my heart.

That is all I have ever wanted.

A year from now I imagine I will have finally saved up enough money to take my dream trip to Europe. I imagine at this very moment a year from now I'll be sitting on a bench in England by a street with no name. My hair lighter, my skin smoother, pencil and paper in hand, I am writing. Always writing. I imagine I'll be older and wiser, and a couple inches closer to figuring it all out.

That's my dream today.

It helps me go to sleep at night.

Yes, it is certain that I have made a realization and it has been a great one at that. How does one measure happiness? It has been the question that I have found myself pondering. I have always assumed that you feel happiness and when it comes there should be a point where it will stay with you always. There have been moments, as I have been writing this, where I thought I had found happiness. I thought I had found the entrance to inner peace and there were simply no exits. I was mistaken.

I am not sure what causes this certain phenomenon, but I know now that happiness isn't a lifetime. It's the moments of happiness you remember. But what is the other left over time I have between these moments? What should be considered happiness? So I am brought back once more to my question, how do you measure happiness? I always waited for the moments when something extraordinary or delightful happened in my life before I would consider myself to be in a happy moment. But are all the other times I have where nothing spectacular happens, and yet I am simply calm and at peace, just time when I am surviving? Or have I mistaken my happiness with joy? Maybe the seconds of happiness occur when you feel nothing at all. Maybe the joy that is felt is mistaken for happiness, because happiness is so hidden. The moments of calm, of peace, of just being alive,

That is happiness.

Today I walked to the mailbox and got the mail. It was snowing these large flakes that stuck to my body. I tilted my head to look at the world. Today the wind blew at my hair and I closed my eyes to feel it. I looked at my family today and smiled. I sat in the bathtub and read a romance novel. I listened to a song I loved on the radio and I sang along. I watched a television show that made me cry. I laid on my bed and pondered how I would be in the next five years of my life. I dreamed.

Today I was happy.

142

I sat in my bedroom and watched as the clouds rolled by outside my window,

And I was happy.

Because I have been mistaken.

For when you see your happiness as the little moments in your life,

It changes everything.

I met the loneliest man on earth yesterday. He was causally drunk out of mind. I stood next to him as he told me all the reasons for the destruction of hope in this life. He was in so much pain. It was as thick as the liquor on his breath. He was so lonely and the unhappiness crowded his senses.

He cried there for me.

Through his glassy eyes I saw that he had given up.

He chose the pain and the destruction.

He chose death.

In years time he will be dead and I imagine only a hand full of people will care,

For he is already dead.

But he was not all the pain and hopelessness to me,

He was me.

After a few drinks, he told the truth about himself and his life, but he revealed who I was too and who everyone truly is. As odd as it may sound, I found myself understanding his words. I saw that he was afraid, that he was wounded and lonely. I saw that he couldn't stop. I saw he wanted to be understood but he didn't understand himself.

Everyone stood and stared at him with one eyebrow cocked,

"Messed up alcoholic fuck." They thought.

They told me not to fall for his tears. They told me not to worry about him.

"His guilt is cheap. He'll do it again."

He was a cheater, a liar, and a womanizer. He was the smartest man by daylight and an alcoholic by night.

He was indeed a messed up fuck.

But I couldn't seem to walk away from him as everyone else had. I suppose it was because I couldn't seem to get over the fact that I understood him and

that I am too out of control. Here's the thing, if you put thirty people in the room that knew me they would tell you that I'm wonderful.

The truth is that I lied to their face.

No one knows or could truly understand the dark caves and alleys that weave themselves through me. No one knows the darkness that creeps hidden from the eyes.

Everyone is afraid to speak of it.

I hide mine from the world, but this man was saying and acting what everyone in this world was. The lonliness and sorrow. The bad days, the sleepless nights, the endless tears, the lost love and the consent fall.

He was me too.

My confession to you: I'm a liar and I'm a cheater. I'm a snake and I am certainly a bitch. I will be a back stabber if it will give me something that I want. Sometimes I enjoy hurting people because it makes me feel good. I cry helplessly, even though I don't deserve anyone's sympathy. And though I may not be an alcoholic or a drug addict. I am addicted to so many other things that bring me that high I need.

And you know what?

I can't stop either.

I am addicted to the satisfaction of other people's pain because I want to be the one to be noticed and I want to be the best. I am addicted to the scale and the compliments because I have no self-worth. I am addicted to the sorrow because I am afraid to be happy. I am addicted to fanaticizing about other girl's boyfriends wanting me. I secretly try to catch their attention because I am jealous of people who have someone who loves them and who are happy. I am addicted to the opposite sex because I figure if I can't figure out myself out maybe they can. I am addicted to the dreams because I am scared to make it all a reality. I am addicted to the anger because it is

145

the only thing that makes me feel passionate. I am addicted to criticizing because I love to bring everyone down around me.

And that is just the beginning of the addictions I have.

We are all addicted to things that make us feel good about ourselves and our lifes even though they only bring us that aching pain in the end.

The temporary highs.

So it turns out that we all are messed up fucks.

Some of us are better at hiding it than others. Some of us can't hide it at all.

As I looked and understood that man I realized that I was too dying.

Soon I will be dead,

And no one will care that I existed.

All because of the simple fact that I have decided to hide from the truth.

What has my life done when I have been lost in this endless despair that consumes me completely?

Nothing, absolutely nothing.

I knew at that moment I needed to change, not just speak of it. I needed to look at my life and see it as it truly was and then finally make the corrections that I have been afraid to make.

And I cried the same tears as that man.

I choose to care about those who are looked down upon even though that may result in me being looked down upon myself.

I choose to change.

I choose the truth.

I choose to fight this sorrow.

I choose to save myself from this drowning.

I choose redemption.

I choose life, not the death of a life.

I choose life.

And so I wonder what it would be like to jump off the top of K-Mart and let my brains splatter on the sidewalk. The local news station would have a great story then. "Who knows the reasons why anyone could do this to themselves? "They would say to the camera as they stood by my lifeless body.

There are billions of reason why I could jump off the top of K-Mart, but what I think I'm trying to say is there is a voice that exists in my soul that says, "Maybe not today. I bet tomorrow is going to be better." And so I don't just give up. For all the reasons I have to throw myself off the roof of K-Mart, I have at least a couple more better reasons to live.

Someday I'm going to be a lover. I'm going to be a mother, a best friend, a sister-in-law, and a grandmother. I'm going to be a wife and a caregiver. Someday I'm going to save the world. So why would I give up now when I have so much to live for?

There is so much here, if you open your eyes, there is just so much.

I am running out of paper in this notebook.

Sometimes I feel like I'm running out of time.

If you had one chance to change your life, would you?

I feel like I am at a crossroad.

Be what they want and what is expected of me,

Or be what I want to be.

This is it.

This is the time and there is no other time.

When everything stays or I decide to change.

I've only got one chance.

Can I tell you a secret?

I have always imagined that once I found my place in the world, once I found a home, a love, and the peace of mind I've been searching for all my life, I would make myself a New York style cheesecake. Then I would sit outside, look at the night sky and my life, and eat my cake.

You know what?

I bet it's going to be the best cheesecake I ever had.

I woke up today to find that my skin looked smoother than the day before. I watched the television and everyone was smiling their white teeth at me.

The economy is shit but everyone is dancing anyway.

I put on high heels and walked around in my pajamas. I danced on my bed and listened only to happy music on the radio.

The sun smiled at me.

I forgot about my problems. I forgot about men. I forgot about my conquest to conquer the world.

I just am alive today.

I watched Saturday Night Live and ate a bowl of ice cream without feeling guilty.

Yes, that's right,

It was a Goddamn beautiful day,

And I was right in the middle of it all.

I sat outside and looked at the constellations that were the most beautiful things I had ever seen.

Wish you could have been there.

Hopeless body of mine, I think I still love you even if nobody else may.
Though you may be a size ten with crooked big toes, I think you are just fine
as you are.

Maybe I like myself this way.

Maybe I am beautiful just as I am today.

Can you see it now?

What lies underneath the clothes and the skin I have.

I have learned through my own pain that there is so much more than just
layers of the skin.

Underneath all skin lies a soul and this is where a life lives.

Within this life lives a love.

This love has an ability.

This ability can make you free.

I am free.

I have the ability to love myself just as I am.

I ran naked across my backyard and I let my laughter howl through the sky.
So I am free because I have wiped the fog off the mirror and looked at the
reflection and agreed that I am more than just skin.

I feel an awakening in this skin of mine.

It's about time, don't you think?

On June 28th 2003, I went to Harmony Grounds, which is a place everyone calls the coffee shop, for the first time. I stepped in and was struck immediately by the steam and fragrance of music and people. I sat at the bar with a friend and asked for a hot chocolate. I sat there and glanced at the world around me.

There was a band playing. Two guitar players and a drummer. This one guitar player had this hat on, and immediately I was drawn to him. It was like he was trying to hide something. I am too trying to hide something. I wish you could have been there to see him play. He looked so alive every time he played a note. I looked at him and I wanted him. Odd, it wasn't because I knew him at all, infact, I still have no clue who he really was. It's just that I wanted to feel the way he was feeling at that moment.

Total and complete happiness.

As I sat there I felt no fears, infact, I felt nothing at all. I wasn't empty but I wasn't full. And at the time I was okay because I closed my eyes and listened to the music play and it took me away. I closed off the world and felt nothing.

Long after I had left the coffee shop, and long after I gave that guitar player one last hopeful glance, I stood outside of my house at night. Some moments in life I don't think are suppose to be good or bad. Some moments are designed to give you time to let down your guard and just be.

The moment just was,

That's all.

I looked to the land around me that was covered with darkness and I wished that that guitar player would appear and play a song for me so I could feel alive, but I know I'll never see him again. He was only meant to be there for my moment. To make me feel okay and make me realize that I can love

still and that I am now done hiding. The music was there to remind me that
I still can have peace.

The moment was.

I just was.

And knew that I would have to wake up the next morning to be more.

Sat on my bed and cried today. I think I have spent the last five years of my life crying for reasons that I still don't understand. I think I can remember the moment it all started. I think I can remember every moment in between. Five pathetic years of my life where I wished so much I ached. All I wanted was to change. I tried so hard and every time I failed I would lay on the floor and weep with a hollow grief.

I couldn't seem to get up.

Lately, I feel like I've been letting go. I feel like I've let it slowly slip through my fingers and I watched it all fall away. And something inside feels clear.

I used to be so ashamed of all these words. All the emotions and darkness I have never told anyone before.   .

And I feel so much,

Like I have stepped on a mountain and cried my name to the skies.

Like I'm cleaning out the dust.

Like I'm free.

Like I'm okay.

I looked at myself in the mirror today and I think that maybe I'm doing all right.

I'm okay.

I was twelve when I think it all truly began. I let it build up until I couldn't take it anymore. I can remember the first emotions. The first signs that I was entering into something bigger than me. I was ashamed and I felt all alone. But in the end maybe I was mean to do all of this alone. A twelve year old girl suddenly becomes an eighteen year old woman and she made it through on her own. I've been thinking lately that maybe I am strong. What is it? This thing I have went through? Does it have name? Do you know what I'm talking about? I used to think I was the way I was for one reason, but now I see that there are so many reasons why people lose themselves. I kept it all in for so long, so long, and it took me years to get it out.

Are you caught in the middle of one right now? It's going to be okay, you know that right? I used to think that I wanted to be great but now I realized that you have to be okay before you can move on. For the first time in my life I truly think I'm okay.

I wanted to find out who I was. Funny thing? I always knew exactly who I was. But just encase you're wondering it for yourself the person you are is the person you dream yourself to be, and everything you know for sure.

I shit you not.

You're just too scared and so certain that the world wouldn't let you be the person you wanted to be. You lie to yourself and everyone around you so you don't know what the truth is. Everyone was cruel to you when you did try, so you stopped trying.

I feel like I have washed upon a shore. Aching and tired, I look around at the world and I'm okay. And I'm alive, I'm alive. I sit outside on the porch and let the world hit me in the soul. And I breathed. Now it's time for me finally to become the person I am truly meant to be.

These last few years were just me letting go of the pain I kept. Before that I think I am going to take a while just to be alive. These tears fall down my cheeks and mark the paper, but these are different tears.

Because I'm okay for once,

I'm okay.

I woke up early and drove to Petoskey. The early sun gleamed dimly in the light blue sky as though it was yawning from a deep sleep. I rolled down the window but put on no music, I just wanted it to be silent around me. I got out of my car in the downtown area and walked toward the park that contained a pier that looked out unto the water. I passed a young girl that had long brown hair and these large blue eyes. She sat on a black bench staring at me. I walked on past the docks where my grandfather used to fish. I saw a dark shadow of a man with his fishing pole, the wind blew gently, and he was gone. I walked on from the swing sets to a woman dancing on the grass. She wore a red dress and a smile that lit the world around her. She wore my red high heel shoes. A woman now, she faced her head to the sky and closed her eyes so she could just feel.

I felt it too, but before I went to join her, I went to the pier and stood at the end of it. The cement and stone met the water and everything went on, but I could not see the end. I stood on that pier until I felt safe to leave. The wind gently swirled around me and I was gone.

Suddenly, I became someone else.

Someone new.

Everything has the ability to change.

I know that now. It changed because I have tried.

I suppose this is just the beginning of the story, even though this is the end of this book. I still have this summer before college starts and I have a great understanding that even though I don't know exactly what life is for sure, I have hope and I will never stop trying and searching for the truths in me and in this world.

I started writing this because I thought this was about a certain point in my life where everything went wrong, but I realized that I needed to take this time to look at my life completely. For the very first time, I examined the contents within me and I have found something so great inside those contents that I swear I will never let go of.

When I was on that pier I placed my hand in the water and felt something wash away. I realized that every tear I ever cried helplessly, every prayer I had whispered at night, every moment when I couldn't breathe, every morning I woke up dead, meant nothing anymore. Every moment I realize now is only mine, and I have changed because I have tried. I am alive by writing this, because these words make me free.

And I am finally free,

And I am okay.

For today I was born again and I will never let life slip away. I've been thinking that I am so close to my joy, and when I find it I am going to have so much to talk about. Will you listen? But for now I am just breathing and that is all I needed.

I finally put on my dress with my red high heels today,

And I raised my head to the sky.

It seems I had forgot about life.

I forgot about love and forgiveness.

I forgot that I had the strength to do anything.

This life, my life, is now on the way.

That is one thing I know for sure.

I walk away for now, a dim light surrounding me.

I forgot about life, but you shouldn't.

As you hold this page in your hand,

How do you feel?

Am I so off or can you relate to me?

Wouldn't it be nice if we could just figure out this life?

Until that day here's a toast,

To the pain and the way things used to be,

To the love,

To the happiness and way things are going to be.

Maybe someday it'll all make sense,

But for now I am walking on.

One last glance, I walk to the horizon.

But this is not the end,

There is never an end with this story of life.

The reason I wrote this:

It's hard to say really. I thought it was for myself but then I thought about all the people who would read it. My advice to them would be to go to Wal-Mart and pick up a cheap notebook and start writing. Write about life. This is the only way you will find out how you lost it.

And when you find life again, I am telling you, the joy is so great.

You'll find this happiness, and I swear it feels just like a sunrise

Life can be so surprising sometimes.

Do you hear it?

It's echoing now and it is so beautiful.

Can you finally hear me now?

As I walked on, I had to keep myself from shattering. I heard a voice call from the sky and I drank the moment in deeply. I lifted my head to the stars and I wondered with all the depths of my soul.

I wondered,

Because I wonder about this life.

If you would like to e-mail the author of this book you can send your message to thewonderinglife7@yahoo.com.